Fundamentals of
Preaching

—JOHN KILLINGER—

Fundamentals of Preaching

FORTRESS PRESS   PHILADELPHIA

Library of Congress Cataloging in Publication Data

Killinger, John.
  Fundamentals of preaching.

  Bibliography: p.
  Includes index.
  1. Preaching.   I. Title.
  BV4211.2.K53   1985   251   84–47926
  ISBN 0–8006–1796–7 (pbk.)

K967F84   Printed in the United States of America   1–1796

FOR MY SON ERIC
with love and pride as
he begins his
journey in ministry

Contents

Introduction

Preaching, at its best, is not a solo task. It is done by an individual, but it is the sum of many things — of the community of faith, the Bible the community holds at its center, the tradition of proclamation it has nurtured, and the gifts, experiences, and artifices of the preacher. Therefore it is not a subject that can be imparted in a book, even if the book is a large one. It is something that must be felt, imbibed, studied, lived. It grows by reflection, listening, prayer, reappraisal, constant effort. And, in the end, no one can really judge its value, for it is not an end in itself. It exists to point people to Christ and the kingdom — even though the kingdom is already within them.

These words are said to provide a setting for a book such as this. They remind the reader that no book can be a final arbiter of what preaching is and how it should be done. As the author, I have no illusions about that. In my lifetime I have read literally hundreds of books about preaching, heard most of the great preachers of our time, and worked with several of them. Yet every sermon is still a new experience for me, a chartless journey upon the seas of life and death. There are tricks of the trade, habits of mind, a residue of experience; but every sermon worth its salt is a fresh creation, an unrepeated — and unrepeatable — adventure.

So how does one presume to write a book about preaching? It is, I suppose, an act of unmitigated gall, even more than that required for the act of preaching itself. If one rarely preaches the same way twice but sets out on a new journey in each sermon, how can he or she hope to instruct others in the art of doing it?

Perhaps the book itself is like a sermon — that is, it is an adventure, a journey, a setting out on the way. The reader goes along, as the hearer of a sermon goes along, and while not becoming a replicate of the writer, participates in the adventure and has experiences of his or her own that justify the traveling. Some will follow carefully, absorbing details and discovering nuances that not even the author knew were there. Others, like some sermon tasters one has known, will dip into the material here and there, the way a well-thrown flat stone skips upon the water from place to place. And who is to say that the latter will not have profited more than the former? For what one receives from either a sermon or a book usually depends on what one has brought to the occasion by way of preparation or mood or motivation to learn.

At any rate, as I was leaving fifteen years of teaching in a seminary and returning to the parish, I felt that I had to write the book. It seemed only fitting, if only as a swan song to my academic career. Surely out of all those years of counseling with students about their sermons and of reading and lecturing about preaching, I had something important to say about my subject matter and would not turn out like the Orator at the end of Ionesco's *The Chairs*, who stood to summarize an old man's philosophy of life after the old man had just leaped from the window to his death, and was a mute incapable of anything more than garbled noises! So I wrote the first draft of the book in my final semester of teaching and then packed it away in my files, where it remained for the better part of two years as I was getting settled in my new work.

As I now write these words of introduction and prepare to undertake the revision of my manuscript, I feel very positive about this lapse of time. It means that the book will be a book about preaching by a professor of preaching, who is supposed to know all there is to know about such things, revised by a parish minister, who knows what it is really like to be on the firing line every Sunday. I frankly cannot say at the outset how much will be changed, but I can promise that the result will be honest and practical, for I intend to strike down every false sentiment and high-flown idea I find in it! Theory and practice, I hope, will come together in a useful way, and the reader, whether a careful follower or a skipping stone, will be given a faithful tour through one man's process of preparing his sermons.

1

The Tradition of Preaching

The preacher of the gospel is not doing something new, however original he or she may feel. Ecclesiastes was right: there is nothing new under the sun. The ancients stole all of our best ideas.

The nation of Israel was formed by preaching and sustained by it. *Shema, Israel*, "Hear, O Israel." Like a tent pole, the proclamation rose in the midst of the people, defining their center and their being. When they listened and were faithful, they were the community of God. When they didn't, they were "no people," as Hosea called them, or "not my people." It was that simple.

They loved to hear the history of their relationship to God — of the calling of Abram, the birth of a son from Sarah's ancient womb, the near-sacrifice of Isaac, the wiliness of Jacob, the selling of Joseph, the rise of Moses, the years in the wilderness, the taking of Jericho, the selection of Saul, the greatness of David. Recital theology, it has been called, ticking off the things God had done for them and to them and through them. Call it preaching, if you please, or proclaiming. The effect was to sustain a nation, to revive Israel, as both fact and idea, from generation to generation.

Put your ear to the Old Testament and listen. You will hear it, like the murmur of the sea, all the way through: the recitative, the same phrases played over and over.

> God took us when we were slaves,
>   gave us leaders,
> and brought us to this land,
>   which he enabled us to subdue.

4

> Even in the wilderness
>   he formed us as a people,
>   giving us his Torah.
> When we cleave faithfully to him,
>   caring for the poor and weak among us,
> he blesses us with peace and victory.
> When we disobey, and seek our own way,
>   he chastizes us.
> Truly he is a great God;
>   his covenant is forever,
>   and we are his people.

Listen! Don't you hear it — in the Pentateuch, in Joshua, in Samuel and Kings and Chronicles, in all the prophets, in the devotional writings? Hear, O Israel — listen to the preaching — and the community is formed.

It is little wonder that the New Testament reveals a similar rehearsal-to-form-the-community among early Christian preachers. The sermons of the Book of Acts are framed on such a schema. So are the homiletical sections of Paul's letters, the parts where he forgot himself and raised his voice, where he stopped meddling and went to preaching.

Professor C. H. Dodd has caught the essence of this kerygma or preaching outline in his little book *The Apostolic Preaching*. Here, he says, is the heart of Paul's message:

> The prophecies are fulfilled, and the new Age
>   is inaugurated by the coming of Christ.
> He was born of the seed of David.
> He died according to the Scriptures, to deliver us
>   out of the present evil age.
> He was buried.
> He rose on the third day according to the Scriptures.
> He is exalted at the right hand of God, as Son of God
>   and Lord of quick and dead.
> He will come again as Judge and Saviour of men.[1]

The outline wasn't Paul's alone, of course, or even Paul's first. He was always quick to remind his hearers that he invented none of it, that he preached what he had received, what had been given to him by others. That in itself attests to the centrality of such a kerygma among the early Christians. It was no overturning of the

5

Old Testament kerygma, but a fulfillment of it. It was a modern redaction, an updating of the acts of God in the present age. Nor was that the last of it.

Redactionism doesn't stop. The tradition *lives*; that is, it grows dynamically. By the Middle Ages, it was necessary to remember that God had blessed his community so greatly that it was in all the world, with its center at Rome instead of Jerusalem. After the Reformation, people recalled what God had done through Wyclif and Hus and Zwingli and Calvin and Luther, how his Word had been made available in common print so everyone who could read at all could read it in his or her own language. After the evangelical movement of the eighteenth century, there were stories that could be told about the way the Spirit had anointed the hearts and tongues of farmers, coal miners, and industrial workers. Perhaps the great story of our time, however, is about the social gospel — the way the compassion of Christ has entered agencies and institutions far beyond the walls of the church. There is always a new word being added, because the acts of God go on and on. And when the Word is declared the tent pole goes up, the community is formed. Hear, O Israel. God is doing his work in our midst.

This is why the preacher must never regard himself or herself as a loner. We preach in a great succession of preachers, in a line stretching all the way back to the apostles, and, before them, to the prophets of Israel.

I recall sitting one pleasant summer morning under the enormous wooden tabernacle at Chautauqua Institute, nervously waiting for the moment when I must stand and speak. The size of the congregation unsettled me. What did I have to say to them? How could I measure up to their expectations, or worse, up to their needs? I stared at the floor behind the pulpit. It was worn in an obvious pattern by the feet of those who had stood at the pulpit through the years: Bishop Vincent (founder of Chautauqua), DeWitt Talmadge, Dwight L. Moody, William Jennings Bryan, Harry Emerson Fosdick, Ralph Sockman, George Buttrick, Paul Scherer (who was a perennial favorite and had a house nearby). I thought of them standing there, shuffling their feet in nervousness and then in eagerness as their passion rose and they endeavored to make their points. I felt a surge of confidence at the

6

thought of standing where they had stood, speaking the word they spoke. The great cloud of witnesses, and I was only the most recent.

Fittingly, I remembered a paragraph I had once read about the British clergyman G. A. Johnston Ross when he was invited to be one of the first preachers in the restored abbey at Iona, the ancient Christian community founded by St. Columba in the sixth century. Said Ross:

> As I took my place at the little temporary pulpit beside the ancient altar base, and looked first at my congregation (composed in part of scientific men from England, in part of the aged fishermen whom I had known as stalwart lads) and then through the glassless windows at the burial place of sixty-six of our Scottish and Norwegian kings and earls, whose bodies a thousand years ago had been brought there because of the sanctity of the holy isle, there swept over me (need you wonder?) an awe of the Eternal who had labored so long within the aspirations of men. . . . What I preached that day is long ago forgotten, as is most meet; but I shall never forget what I *was* that day—consciously the child of the centuries and of the variegated grace of God which they carried. All petty provincialism was impossible: the broken altar base, the stern lift of the walls, the presence of the august dead forbade. And this elevation of soul and broadening of view do come to the men who appreciate the presence of God in the community of faith.[2]

Community is, after all, what it's about. We are part of a great community. We are building a great community. We do not stand on our own platform when we preach, but on the community's. We do not invite people to join ourselves, but the community which is initiated by God, called by God, sustained by God, served by God.

Recognizing this makes a great difference in what we preach and in how we approach the task of preaching. It banishes our fears. It identifies our audience. It determines our message. It guarantees our success.

We have this treasure, said Paul—*this inestimable treasure*—in earthen jars—*fragile pottery, not very good for the ages*—in order that the glory may belong to God—*who is not fragile and is building his community forever.*

There is no submerging of the preacher's personality, not for a minute. Even earthenware vessels have their personalities. Phillips Brooks was right: preaching is truth *through* personality. But the individual personality is carried on the waves of the ancient community. It rises to heights it could not reach alone, because it is lifted by the great community, the communion of saints in all the ages.

This fact gives wholeness to the preacher when he or she preaches — the kind of wholeness and virtue the preacher needs to speak the Word of God that continues to call community into existence. It discourages mere cuteness or novelty or folksiness or idiosyncrasy, and condemns personal prejudices and ignorance. It calls for knowledge, discipline, insight, compassion, tolerance, love.

The idea of community is behind Paul's comments on tongues-speaking in 1 Corinthians 12 – 14. If a particular action doesn't build the community, he said — if no one else understands it — then it doesn't merit any place in Christian worship. The community is the test, and the community makes for wholeness: wholeness of theology, wholeness of knowledge, wholeness of purpose, wholeness of passion. This is also why Paul could reduce the matter to a question of love in 1 Corinthians 13. Without love, we are sounding brass, tinkling cymbals, silly wind chimes. Love forms the community, and without it there is no community.

The preacher's first calling, therefore, is to love. Otherwise the preacher doesn't understand community and has nothing to preach. We must love the community and love the people who belong to the community. It is not enough, if one wishes to preach, to be in love with preaching. It is not enough to be in love with the Christian philosophy. It is not even enough to be in love with God. We must love people and love God's vision of the community. Then we can preach.

This is not an easy thing. How does one practice being in love? By going into the jungle as Schweitzer did or into the inner city with the more modern saints? By ministering in the porno alleys and tenement rows, where human life is broken and degraded and cheap? Perhaps that is one way. But life may also be broken and degraded and cheap on Wall Street or in opulently manicured suburbs or Ivy League schools or high-steepled churches. Zimbabwe and Tijuana and Harlem have no corner on brokenness.

There need be no outward rush, in other words, to find love in some exotic setting. Its necessity dwells closer to us than that and, in fact, inhabits people living under the same roof with us, people in the next apartment, the next office, the next seat on the commuter train, or, closer still, ourselves.

We begin to love when we begin to see the human condition and when we sense the horrible, limiting finitude of our lives; when we feel the seething power of ambition, hate, greed, disappointment, and yearning in people all around us. We begin to love when we wish it could be otherwise, that the entire human race could be whole and joyous, that every last one of us could be part of a great family of God in which, as Revelation expresses it, there would be no more tears and no more sorrow, and life would be one extravagant party of loving and sharing and being together in the Spirit.

This is where the gospel comes in and where preaching begins. The gospel didn't have its start in the New Testament with Jesus and Paul. It was already there in the Old Testament and has been there from the beginning. Its word is that God loves us and is forming a community for us. All we have to do is to find ways of joining it.

This is why preaching is an ongoing task. We must find more and more ways of joining the community, of making it happen, of letting God's kingdom come on earth. We are the fragile vessels who will be left behind when the next generation comes along. But for now we have the treasure, the message. And we must learn how to preach it.

NOTES

1. C. H. Dodd, *The Apostolic Preaching and Its Developments* (New York: Harper & Brothers, 1936), p. 17.

2. Quoted in Henry Sloane Coffin, *The Public Worship of God* (Philadelphia: Westminster Press, 1946), pp. 38–39.

—2—

The Importance of the Bible

Proclamation is the task of a community, not merely of an individual. By the same token, the Bible, from which we derive our preaching, is a community book. It belongs to the people of God. The community made it, the community lives by it, the community interprets it. If we wish to represent the community in our speaking, then we must steep ourselves in the pages of the Book.

The greatest preachers have always been lovers of the Bible. Those who have based their preaching on other texts—on the poets, the news media, their own opinions—have passed quickly from the mind, as though they established their ministries on quicksand. The ones who built their sermons on great biblical ideas and passages have lingered in our memories. It is not that they were more original than the others—perhaps to the contrary—but that there is something solid and enduring about the Scriptures, something capable of rescuing even mediocre homiletical minds from transience and obscurity.

The Bible is the community's book, and the minister who would preach must come to love it, must live in its pages day by day and year by year, until it fairly saturates his or her being. He or she should pour over it the way people review old family albums, looking for their roots of existence in the faces and environments of days gone by, and reading the present and the future in the light of the past.

Part of our problem today is that we don't have roots or don't know how to find them. Our society is so new, so mobile, so transient, that we feel rootless and alone. Wyatt Cooper comments on this in *Families*. He says: "We are trying to learn to live today without those roots that in the past afforded us the reassurance of stability, permanence, and continuity. Most of our children could not tell you the names of their grandparents. We have moved into a time when our children can say, with Napoleon's General Junot, that they are their own ancestors."[1] Cooper remembers his boyhood, when he would go with family members to great reunions and listen to tales of relatives who had preceded him. The stories *located* him. They provided him with a history, a past, a sense of community. Once, at a reunion, all the family went out to a family graveyard, where they stood spinning yarns across fallen tombstones and honeysuckle vines. "A child could stand," says Cooper,

> as I stood, with his bare feet digging into the sand of their graves and know that their toil and their despair, their trials and their triumphs, were forever a part of him, just as their dust and their bones were forever a part of the land.
>
> I could see that the world did not begin with me. I could see that I was a part of all that went before, and they, those vanished thousands, are forever a part of what I am and of what I shall be.
>
> It is important for a child to know that. The world does not begin nor end with him, and in between his being born and his dying, he has a link to forge. He has a challenge, a chance, and a responsibility.[2]

Do you see what is wrong with preaching that is not rooted in the community and the community's book? It misses the wholeness, the mystery, the joy. It is like cut flowers that will fade before the evening comes. It cannot absorb and transmit the sense of an agelong struggle to be the people of God, to redeem the environment, to come and worship at the throne of the Holy. It fails, and in its failure breeds despair.

This is not to say that there are not other texts we should occasionally take for our sermons — more recent texts from Luther or Calvin, from Wesley or Wordsworth, from the Berrigans or Martin Luther King, Jr. These are part of our story, too, and using them will remind our congregations that tradition is a living entity, that community is still being formed in our own time.

But the bulk of our work will be with the Bible, for in our community it is the commonly accepted basis of all our understanding. It contains all the great themes found in later writings. They are not always evident at first glance, but they are there. It would be impossible, I believe, to introduce a theme for which one could not find some precedence in the pages of Scripture. What are the pressing issues of our time? *War?* The Bible is full of the problem. *Ecology?* In the books of prophecy it is known as responsibility for the land and, in the New Testament, as stewardship. *Social welfare?* The law, the prophets, and the epistles are full of it. *The disintegration of the home?* Reread Hosea and 1 and 2 Corinthians and the Epistle of James.

Not that all of our answers are to come from the Bible. That is a foolish form of biblicism which denies the nature of the developing community through the ages. But the themes are there, incipient and waiting, so that the thoughtful preacher of the Book can make the connections. It is simply that the Bible is a book about life, and all important subjects, regardless of how modern or technical they are, are reducible to life problems. For this reason, we can never treat any theme in our preaching that has not, in one way or another, found its way into the Scriptures.

CENTERED ON GOD

The most important thing about the community's book is the fact that it is centered on God. Therefore when we treat any life theme or life problem and trace its relationship to a similar theme in the Bible, we inevitably discover its theological dimensions. They all run, like the colored ribbons on a Maypole, to the center of life itself, the Creator/Redeemer of the faithful community.

This is what gives preaching its distinctive character. This is why, in an era of mass-market books, television entertainment, and information overkill, people can still hear an authentic word from the stuttering lips of a mediocre parson in a one-room country church house. The Bible is about the community, but it is also about God. It is about God's struggling with the community through the years, shaping it in an act of creation far more risky and difficult than the creation of the world itself. And talking about God is more important than anything we can do for people. Where else in the world will they hear about God? The preacher who has abandoned talking about God has abandoned our raison d'être, our calling to be proclaimers. When people come to us for help, said Karl Barth, "they do not really want to learn more about *living*: they want to learn more about what is on the farther edge of living — *God*."[3]

How frustrated people are when the preacher talks about world issues without any reference to biblical theology, or discusses some psychological disorder without grounding it in the biblical understanding of persons, or delivers a lecture on marriage or education or the human predicament without tracing its roots in the community's dealings with God.

Years ago, when ships were the only way communications could be carried from the old countries to America, people in America anxious for news from relatives and loved ones would assemble at the dock as soon as a mast was sighted. The moment a gangplank was thrown up and sailors began to disembark, hands would stretch out and cries would go up from the crowd beseeching, "Is there any word? Is there any word?" And I can testify, as one who has often gone to church with the masses of modern men and women who feel isolated, cut off from community, lost in this wasteland of electronics and gadgetry, that we enter the sanctuary with the same plea: "Is there any word?"

When there is — when the Bible is faithfully preached and we, like Faulkner's Dilsey, have seen the Alpha and the Omega, the Beginning and the End — we go away with a glow in our hearts, with a feeling that we can get our acts together again for living triumphantly in a hard environment. When there isn't — when the preacher has dallied with some trifling idea or sentiment and has clearly had no word for himself or herself — we slink away like quarry slaves bound for our prisons another week.

It is always tempting for an educated preacher to deliver personal opinions. The greater the education, the greater the temptation. But it is the Bible that speaks most clearly and authoritatively to people's needs — especially when one reads the Bible critically, with a theological eye to its major themes and interests.

It should be instructive to us that the Reformation which rescued the church from its great decline into moralism and superstition, so that there were preachers who did not preach mere trifles to the world, was first and foremost a recovery of the biblical writings within the beloved community. Martin Luther constantly emphasized the teaching of the Word. He insisted to his preaching students: "Thou must plant thyself upon a clear, transparent, strong statement of the Scriptures, whereby thou canst then hold thy ground."[4] And Roland Bainton has reminded us of how electrifying it was for Zwingli's congregation in Zurich to hear him Sunday after Sunday expounding from an open Greek Bible on the pulpit before him. One young humanist in the audience, Thomas Platter, said he felt as if he were being lifted by the hair of his head. Platter was so excited by the gospel that he supported himself as a manual laborer by day in order to study Greek at night, and studied with sand in his mouth in order that the gritting in his teeth would keep him awake. "The news of the discovery of America," says Bainton, "had produced no such excitement."[5]

CHOOSING A TEXT

How does one go about preaching a biblical sermon? It is possible to do so, if one is fairly saturated with biblical concepts, without actually speaking from a specific text, just as it is possible, if one is not thus saturated, to employ a text and then preach a non-biblical sermon. Merely quoting the Bible is no guarantee of doing biblical preaching. Some of the most ignorant and misleading preaching one hears is peppered with scriptural quotations. But normally the preacher who wishes to preach biblically will launch his or her sermon from a particular segment of Scripture. This has the advantage, if the segment is faithfully dealt with, of providing a biblical focus to the sermon; and it may, unless the sermon is given as a mere exposition or running commentary on the text, provide valuable hints about the shape the sermon should assume.

There are two principal ways of approaching the sermon that is based on a primary text. One is to begin with an idea or a topic for the sermon and then to go to the Bible for a strong text in support of it. The other is to begin with the text itself, chosen either from one's reading in the Scriptures or from a lectionary which contains designated readings for each Sunday.

1. *Beginning with an idea or a topic.* This has been a favored method of many great preachers. Most of them have kept notebooks in which they have entered the seminal ideas, notions, and inspirations that occurred to them while reading, talking with people, or simply reflecting on life. These sermon "germs" would eventually sprout and begin to bring forth the entire sermon. During the seasoning time, the homiletical mind would be turning over its knowledge of the Scriptures, asking such questions as: "What passage challenges or supports this notion of mine?" "Which biblical character has experienced this same problem in another form?" Then, by the time the sermon was ripe for picking, its rootage would be deep into the veins of the Scriptures.

Harry Emerson Fosdick, who was one of the most important preachers in American history, always used this approach in preparing sermons. Early in his ministry he discovered that his most fruitful preaching was done in response to the many needs he encountered in parishioners during counseling sessions. His ideas or sermon "germs" came from his counseling. Fortunately, as students of Fosdick's sermons know, his preaching on these topics was solidly grounded in biblical faith. His sermons may have been problem-oriented, but they were also God-centered. Otherwise they would not have proven helpful to people. "I had been suckled on the Bible, knew it and loved it," wrote Fosdick in his autobiography, "and I could not deal with any crucial problem in thought and life without seeing text after text lift up its hands begging to be used. The Bible came alive to me — an amazing compendium of every kind of situation in human experience with the garnered wisdom of the ages to help in meeting them."[6]

For a biblically oriented mind like Fosdick's, this method was superb. But too many preachers, not suckled on the Bible as he was, have no such clamor of texts reaching out to them. Or if they reach out, it is unbeknown to the preacher, who sails away from port on some flimsy bark of a text while dozens of sturdier ones languish in the water behind!

2. *Beginning with the text itself.* This is the surer method, espe-

cially for the younger or less experienced preacher. The preacher chooses a text on his or her own, based on a personal study of the Scriptures, or follows the selection of a lectionary, which arranges the major portions of the Bible for planned reading in a three- or four-year cycle. There is particular advantage to the lectionary method, for it keeps the preacher always moving into new areas of thought and doctrine, or what George Buttrick called "the full orbit of the faith," instead of permitting him or her to settle down in favorite ruts.

I always insisted to my students in preaching classes that they spend at least their first five years preaching from lectionary texts and then decide whether to abandon or to continue the method. This would give them time, I felt, to learn much more about the Bible and to become maturer theologians before any of them opted to begin preaching out of their own ideas and experiences. Most of them, I learned, chose to stay with the lectionary. They discovered that it gave them more freedom in preaching than they had when they were responsible for a new topic every week. It also gave them a stronger sense of the community behind the book, because they knew that the texts from which they preached were being used in thousands of other pulpits on the same Sundays.

STUDYING THE TEXT

Whether the preacher employs the texts that leap out for attention or the ones suggested by a lectionary, it is important that he or she study each text carefully before attempting to organize a sermon on it. Much preaching fails at this initial stage because preachers often assume that they know the meanings of texts they have read and used before. They slip into old texts the way one slips into a comfortable pair of house shoes and flap through a sermon that is neither more nor less than the other sermons they have delivered on the same text. What is missing is the fire of fresh spadework, of rethinking, of new insights.

In order to establish the self-will of a particular text—to hear it in any approximation of its fullness and trenchancy—it is often necessary to refresh oneself on the various themes and subthemes of an entire book of the Bible. The preacher cannot escape the fact that each book is a literary composition and that as such it is governed by certain internal rules and agendas. To miss these — to forget their tone and orientation — is often to miss the real thrust of a passage within the book. Mark 16:1-8, for example, which narrates the appearance of the women at the tomb of Jesus and their failure to tell the disciples about the resurrection because they were afraid, seems enigmatic and unsatisfying as an Easter passage until one recalls the constant theme in Mark of the blindness of the disciples to what Jesus was trying to teach them; to the very end, they stubbornly missed the point of his messiahship. The text is really a very powerful one for modern audiences because they can so readily identify with people who could not understand the resurrection.

Unfortunately — and often owing to the bad practices of ministers — many people in our congregations view the Bible as a holy repository of isolated sayings and do not know how to read it in a more sensible literary way. If it is to recover its true place in the community, preachers must begin to treat it more responsibly in their sermons. As P. T. Forsyth once said, it is one of the great tasks of any preacher to rescue the central book of our heritage from "the Biblicist, atomist idea which reduces it to a religious scrapbook, and uses it only in verses or phrases." What the preacher must do, he advised, is to "cultivate more the free, large, and organic treatment of the Bible, where each part is most valuable for its contribution to a living, evangelical whole, and where that whole is articulated into the great course of human history."[7]

One excellent way to accomplish a "free, large, and organic treatment" of the text is to preach occasional series on whole books of the Bible. In this manner the preacher can devote time to a full-scale reexamination of a Gospel, an epistle, or a book of prophecy and then develop several sermons that depend on that single study effort. The authors' themes can be highlighted for the congregation week after week, so that people begin to perceive the importance of serious biblical study over occasional, piecemeal investigations.

Of all the books a preacher should purchase in these days of alluring dust jackets and advertisements, none are more important than biblical commentaries, theological word books, and studies in biblical theology. These are the books that will retain their value, that will become dog-eared and spine-worn through the years, for they do not go quickly out of date. It was these that old Alexander Whyte meant when he leaned over his students, as A. J. Gossip recalls, "with his whole soul in his face, imploring us to sell our bed, and buy this or that book."[8] It is also helpful to own the great volumes on biblical culture such as Johannes Pedersen's monumental *Israel*, W. D. Davies's *Paul and Rabbinic Judaism*, and Raymond Brown's *Jesus and the Beloved Community*. These help to build a feeling for the times, a context for understanding and interpretation.

A WORD OF WARNING

The preacher should thoroughly study a text before attempting to preach on it. But how much of the study should actually show in the sermon? A great lawyer once said that a good legal counselor reveals in the courtroom only 20 percent of the careful study he or she has done in preparation for a trial; any more than that, he said, would turn both judge and jury against him. This is perhaps a healthy reminder for the preacher. People do not respond favorably to pedantry, to the unnecessary display of erudition.

A few preachers are infected by "academicitis." They are so proud of their biblical knowledge that they feel compelled to share it with the congregation, down to the final jot and tittle. They frequently tell people more than people want to know about a subject, especially if it is some remote topic from antiquity. As Fosdick observed, "Only the preacher proceeds still upon the idea that folk come to church desperately anxious to discover what happened to the Jebusites."[9]

The scholarship should be there; it should lie like steel girders beneath the presentation of the sermon. But it need not poke out at odd angles all over the structure, as if some capricious architect had taken it into his head to display what costly materials had gone into the substructure. Sketch enough of a biblical background to show the relationship of the text to its environment, but don't bore the congregation with details of composition and archaeology that are extraneous to the thrust and movement of the sermon.

Do be honest about the text. You need not go out of your way to display critical problems that have no great bearing on it; as George Sweazey says, "Honesty does not require a minister to say, 'Let us pray the Lord's Prayer, adding at the end those words that are not his.'"[10] But it is important that you be open and critical in your approach to the Scriptures, so that people learn from you a proper approach for themselves.

Leander E. Keck says in *The Bible in the Pulpit*[11] that preachers have systematically eliminated the excitement from the Scriptures by trying to homogenize them, or at least by harmonizing them, so that people no longer see the human side of the writers or understand that there are unresolvable contradictions within the holy pages. Therefore people no longer want to study the Bible. The difference between the way the Bible is and the way it has been treated, says Keck, is the difference between the actual coastline of a continent, with all its little inlets and bays, and a large-scale map of the continent that smooths out all the irregularities. The thrill of biblical study comes as we ply the coastline in a small boat, investigating the irregularities, not as we look at the map.

It is vital for persons in the congregation today to see that the faith of Israel and the early church was not given to our forebears without pain and struggle and that those forebears were not perfect human beings. Otherwise they have a mistaken notion of the pilgrimage we are on, or of the importance of our mission in it. They need to see that the community of God is, and has always been, only partially formed and that it is our calling to give it embodiment in our time, working and straining at it as our forebears did.

They will not see any of this unless we are open and honest in our treatment of the Scriptures.

LISTENING TO THE WORD

We cannot leave the matter of the text, even temporarily, without saying something about the preacher's personal appropriation of the word to be heard. It is one of the dangers of our profession that the necessity of handling the Scriptures can easily lead to callousness toward them, so that we ourselves miss the very trumpet sounds our congregations hear.

Therefore it is a good idea, when you are first reading any text, and again afterward when the study has been done and you are rereading it with new appreciation, to set yourself before the Bible as though you were a lost and lowly traveler waiting for a word of redirection. What Denney once said of his friend Struthers of Greenock about the way he read the Scriptures in public ought to be said of us in our private readings: "He never reads Scripture as if he had written it; he always reads it as if listening for a Voice."[12] The Voice is important. If we miss it, we shall not preach well. The apostles were powerful witnesses because they had been overtaken by the Spirit in their own lives, not because they knew anything of homiletics or communications.

Wait silently over the page when you have read it. Close your eyes and let the images cross your mind in vivid retrospect. Let yourself tremble before the presence of the Word in the word. Then, armed with all your commentary background and dictionary knowledge, you will go off to the pulpit with something extra—with the conviction that you yourself have heard the distant echoes of a "Thus saith the Lord." You will feel what Forsyth often said he felt: that while you are by principle on the side of the critics, you have "some difficulty in not believing in verbal inspiration."[13]

And the difference it makes for your people has been well expressed by Thomas Keir: "On the hearer's side the difference is between hearing a sermon and hearing the Word of God; between seeing the forked lightning on a film, and being exposed to the whip and terror of the thing itself; between reading an article about life in the army and being handed your call-up papers; between discussing a dogma and meeting the living God."[14]

NOTES

1. Wyatt Cooper, *Families* (New York: Bantam Books, 1976), p. 99.
2. Ibid., p. 105.

3. Karl Barth, *The Word of God and the Word of Man* (New York: Harper & Brothers, Harper Torchbooks, 1957), p. 189.

4. Martin Luther, *Works*, Erlangen edition, vol. 28, p. 223.

5. Roland Bainton, *The Reformation of the Sixteenth Century* (Boston: Beacon Press, 1952), pp. 82–83.

6. Harry Emerson Fosdick, *The Living of These Days* (New York: Harper & Brothers, 1956), p. 95.

7. P. T. Forsyth, *Positive Preaching and the Modern Mind* (London: Independent Press, 1957), p. 19.

8. A. J. Gossip, *In Christ's Stead* (London: Hodder & Stoughton, 1925), p. 85.

9. Harry Emerson Fosdick, "What Is the Matter with Preaching?" in *Harry Emerson Fosdick's Art of Preaching: An Anthology*, ed. Lionel Crocker (Springfield, Ill.: Charles C. Thomas, 1971), p. 30.

10. George Sweazey, *Preaching the Good News* (Englewood Cliffs, N.J.: Prentice-Hall, 1976), p. 39.

11. Leander E. Keck, *The Bible in the Pulpit* (Nashville: Abingdon Press, 1978).

12. Adam Burnet, *Pleading with Men* (London: Hodder & Stoughton, 1935), p. 102.

13. Forsyth, *Positive Preaching and the Modern Mind*, p. 26.

14. Thomas Keir, *The Word in Worship* (London: Oxford University Press, 1962), p. 133.

---3---

The Personal Dimension

Preaching has several dimensions. It has a *historical* dimension, for it stands in a great tradition reaching back all the way to the early church and beyond that to the prophets of Israel. It has a *biblical* dimension, because the Bible describes the origins of our faith and therefore affects the way we approach any subject or problem today. And it also has a *personal* dimension, for how people hear what we say depends largely on who they are, the experiences they bring to the hearing, and how we are able to use what we know of their identities and experiences to shape our messages.

The fact that preaching exists for people ought not to be easily overlooked. Yet it often is. Some preachers are apparently so impressed by their academic backgrounds or robes of office that they unconsciously believe preaching exists for their sake, as a sublime excuse for delivering pronunciamentos and being seen by hundreds of people while they are doing so. Even congregations can fail to realize that the preaching they are hearing is not doing for them personally what it ought to be doing. If the minister is clever or suave or pious, the people may feel that they are fortunate to have such a minister and never ask themselves, "What is the preacher really saying, and is it important?"

The Gospel of John says that Jesus died because God loved the world, not because God loved a clever pulpit or high-sounding theological phrases or the eleven o'clock hour on Sunday morning. And the preacher who does not also love the world, who does not care deeply and honestly for people, had better rethink the whole matter of ministry. The sermon does not exist to serve God; it exists to serve the people. It is not offered to God as a reminder of how faithful and astute we are; it is offered to the people as a reminder of how faithful and loving God is.

There is, in Samuel Beckett's famous play *Waiting for Godot*, a poor hapless creature named Lucky who is used by the other characters as an ignorant factotum. The two tramps in the play, Didi and Gogo, are fascinated when they learn that Lucky can be made to speak philosophically by putting a hat on his head. When the hat is on, Lucky begins to babble incoherent phrases from the great philosophers of the Western world; when it is taken off he stops. The tramps put the hat on and take it off. On, off. On, off. It is marvelous. Lucky spews out philosophical fragments without even thinking.

Many ministers are like Lucky. They get into the pulpit and begin to spout sermonic material. Then they get out and it is over. But real preaching does not work this way. It is not discontinuous with the work of the pastor. Real preaching grows out of the counseling session, the board meeting, the parish call, the casual encounter in a restaurant or a grocery store. It speaks of and to what the minister has learned in all of his or her dealings with the people during the week. It relates the gospel to human situations and works back and forth between them like a weaver's shuttle.

Preaching that does not do this is not true preaching. It has not understood the nature of the gospel. The gospel cannot be defined by rubrics and doctrines. It is elusive. It takes different shapes in different situations. The preacher who merely talks about rubrics and doctrines, however brilliantly or forcefully, has missed the point. The gospel addresses and assumes the forms of real people's lives or it does not exist at all. It is not theoretical or academic; it is blood and bone, gut and marrow. It speaks to human hurts and hopes, to specific needs and possibilities, or it does not speak at all.

"The preacher needs to be pastor," said Phillips Brooks, "that he may preach to real men."[1] That is, he or she must move in and out among the people, touching them, hearing them, observing them, in order to preach sermons that contain the gospel for them. Otherwise there is no gospel, there is only the pretense of a gospel.

23

Henri Nouwen has put it another way: "Whenever an answer is given when there is no question, support is offered when there is no need, or an idea is given when there is no desire to know, the only possible effect can be irritation or plain indifference."[2] Sermons that exist in and of themselves, without reference to people's pains or joys, are acts of clerical presumptuousness and have no right to be.

William H. Willimon in *Worship as Pastoral Care*[3] underlines the pastoral function of all liturgy. There is something about the great rituals of the church that nourishes people even when they are unaware that it is doing so. Worship comforts, encourages, educates, confronts, converts them. But nowhere in the liturgy is all of this truer than in the sermon. The sermon, together with the prayers, should be the freshest, most contemporaneous part of the service. The sermon ought to be the new patch on an old garment, for it is where the faith is updated and the gospel particularized. It is where individuals hear the "Thou art the man" or "Thou art the woman" of God's latest word. It is where, in Theodore Wedel's word, the gospel becomes *transubstantiated*, so that the symbols of Christ's presence become real flesh and blood for us.

THE IMPORTANCE OF
LISTENING

Most of us assume that preaching consists primarily of speaking. Our earliest associations with sermons, before we have the power of reflection, suggest that to preach means to stand before others and deliver a soliloquy about something, a speech on a religious-sounding topic. We make the same assumption about prayer. Because our first acquaintance with it involves someone's speaking aloud, we take it for granted that prayer is an essentially verbal activity, that one *talks* when one comes before God.

The truth about prayer, of course, is that the most meaningful levels of praying are reached only after one has learned not to speak in the presence of the Holy but to be silent and listen. God comes upon the soul when it is quiet, not when it is chattering. A similar truth exists about preaching – it involves listening, being

24

spoken to, as much as talking. It requires internalizing before there is externalizing, inhaling before there can be exhaling.

There must be listening to God. That is assumed in the character of the minister as a spiritual leader. And there must be listening to the people for whom sermons are prepared. The preacher who listens only to biblical traditions and theological notions, and not to the musings and mutterings of specific human beings who constitute the congregation, is bound to preach irrelevant sermons.

David H. C. Read, in his Warrack Lectures on preaching, described the building plan for an ideal church and manse reported to him by a young minister. The primary feature of the plan was a long corridor leading from the study in the manse to the pulpit in the church. We can imagine it:

> The peaceful study—with the Bible on the desk in the centre, flanked by concordance and commentaries, the walls lined with the best theology, the telephone disconnected, and the door guarded by a zealous wife; and the other door (opened twice on Sundays) with its direct line to the pulpit, the highway for the Word of the Lord, the straight path from the mind of the preacher to the hearts of his hearers. No interruptions, no irrelevancies, no phone calls from Mrs. Brown, no last minute intimations about next Thursday's social, no hawkers, no circulars—the preacher's paradise.[4]

The young man had a lot to learn about life—and about preaching, which draws its inspiration as much from people and their needs as it does from God.

The preacher who is really serious about his or her calling should resolve early on *never to preach a sermon that does not have the clear and statable aim of doing something for people.* The something may vary. It may be to sensitize people to some great moral issue in society. It may be to elicit more compassion in the family or toward one's neighbor. It may be to cause people to reflect on the way they are neglecting their spiritual formation and thus missing the joys of faith. It may be to encourage them in times of widespread despair or pessimism. It may be to prepare them for dying or for facing their grief when loved ones die. The important thing is that the sermon frame an idea, a concept, a

25

message for people, and that this idea, concept, or message be one of genuine significance in their lives.

The only way to guarantee the relevance of the sermon week after week is to be constantly faithful to the task of hearing and knowing what is on people's minds. The good preacher is a good listener. He or she picks up on looks and casual remarks, and probes beneath the surface to learn why people are feeling anxious or lonely or vindictive or happy. A good student of human nature, especially one trained in pastoral psychology, should never want for preaching matter. It abounds in the lives of parishioners. The problem for the sensitive minister is one of inclusion; there are so many things to be preached that one despairs of ever having time to cover them all.

This is as true for the minister who follows a lectionary in preaching as for the one who elects another method. Daily conversations with people in the parish will find resonance in the weekly readings, regardless of the parts of the Bible from which the lections are taken. The minister simply cannot sit down to reflect on a passage of Scripture without being reminded of the problem Mrs. Brown is facing or the remark Mr. Perkins made or the way life is for Mr. and Mrs. Hawkins.

It is a good idea occasionally to make a list of all the personal concerns of the people you have talked to over the past week. If you have a good memory and have been attentive to their conversations, you may be surprised at the length and variety of the list. It will probably contain several of the following items:

Loneliness
Shyness
Fear of failure
Dissatisfaction with a job
Having enough money
Sexual problems
Facing a move
How to raise children
How to express love
Growing old
Caring for others who are aged

Realizing life's great dream
The suffering of the innocent
What happens when one dies
The heaviness of grief
Worries about personal appearance
Dealing with bossy parents
How to be good stewards
Coping with stress
Inferiority feelings
Getting along with others
Feeling stupid or ignorant
Being tired all the time
Learning to live in the present
Being bored

It would be hard to find a decent text anywhere in the Bible that would not reflect at least one of these concerns and offer a chance for pastoral dialogue on it.

Edgar Jackson in *How to Preach to People's Needs* cites a poll that was taken in a large congregation to determine people's ideas of their own needs. Of nearly four thousand replies, half the respondents felt that the major problems of their lives lay within such personal areas as futility, loneliness, insecurity, inferiority, illness, sex, alcoholism, marriage, and guilt feelings. Approximately one-fourth of the persons were concerned with child training, separation, divorce, religious differences in the home, and other marital and domestic problems. The remaining fraction was concerned with social, community, and national problems, or with more traditional religious matters. By figuring averages, says Jackson, it is possible to imagine a cross section of any congregation:

> In a congregation of five hundred people, it is reasonable to assume that at least one hundred have been so recently bereaved as to feel an acute sense of loss. Probably a third of the married persons are facing problems of personality adjustment that may weaken or destroy their home life. At least half of the five hundred can be assumed to have problems of emotional adjustment in school, work,

27

home, or community that endanger their happiness. Others may have neuroses ranging from alcohol addiction to lesser forms of obsessions and anxiety states. Perhaps fifteen or more are homosexually inclined and another twenty-five depressed. Another hundred may be suffering from so great a feeling of guilt or fear of discovery that their peace of mind and health are jeopardized. The rare individual with complete peace of mind and soul is probably surrounded by those who are carrying several heavy burdens within.[5]

How can we, given such a reminder, dare to enter the pulpit without having really listened to our congregations and engaged their concerns in the preparation of our sermons? "A man, to be greatly good," said the poet Shelley, "must imagine intensely and comprehensively; he must put himself in the place of another and of many others; the pains and pleasures of his species must become his own."[6] The same is true for the preacher. We must put ourselves in others' places and see life from where they sit. Otherwise we shall trivialize the gospel by aiming at everything and hitting nothing.

THE NEW SOURCE OF AUTHORITY

Preachers once counted on their authority as ministers to ensure the success of their communication. When they spoke, people listened. But not anymore. The world has become increasingly democratized, and as it has, the whole schematization of authority has changed. Once people at the top of the social hierarchy— rulers, landowners, ministers—spoke and the people under them heard automatically. Now the people at the top retain their authority only by listening to the people under them. Even royal families pay attention to public opinion polls.

If preachers wish to communicate successfully, they must preach dialogically, addressing themselves to the cares and concerns of their congregations. As Fred Craddock has put it, our sermons have to proceed *inductively*, moving from people's interests to the truth of the message, and not *deductively*, beginning with the truth and then applying it to their situations.[7] Instead of posing as authority figures with all the answers, we must struggle for the answers along with our hearers. Instead of appearing in the pulpit with cut-and-dried homilies, we need to come before people in common humanity and work with them toward the conclusions. Then, when we have made the journey together, the conclusions will be personal and inescapable to them.

Reuel Howe perhaps had the knack of it when he suggested that we ought to preach not out of our strengths but out of our weaknesses.[8] That is, we should try to join people where they stand, as much as possible—in doubt and fear and confusion—and work our way from there to a position of illumination and understanding. Among other salutary effects, this would save us from sounding like pompous custodians of eternal truth who have grown tired of our own spiels.

Fosdick anticipated these remarks as long ago as 1928, when he said in an article in *Harper's Magazine*:

> One obvious trouble with the mediocre sermon, even when harmless, is that it is uninteresting. It does not matter. It could as well be left unsaid. It produces this effect of emptiness and futility largely because it establishes no connection with the real interests of the congregation. It takes for granted in the minds of the people ways of thinking which are not there, misses the vital concerns which are there, and in consequence uses a method of approach which does not function. It is pathetic to observe the number of preachers who commonly on Sunday speak religious pieces in the pulpit, utterly failing to establish real contact with the thinking or practical interests of their auditors.[9]

The reason for preaching the sermon in the first place, said Fosdick, "should not be something outside the congregation but inside. Within a paragraph or two after a sermon has started, wide areas of any congregation ought to begin recognizing that the preacher is tackling something of vital concern to them."[10]

PREACHING AS STORYTELLING

One helpful way to conceive of preaching is in terms of the storyteller's art. The good storyteller knows human nature so well that he or she always tells stories that involve the listeners and become their stories. People don't listen to stories because they are fanciful or well told, but because the stories speak to their own needs and conditions. As Bruno Bettelheim has demonstrated in *The Uses of Enchantment*,[11] even the great fairy tales of childhood fulfill deep-seated urges and desires in both children and adults; they represent in disguised form the complexities and difficulties of life and suggest that by cleverness, faithfulness, or innocence one may eventually triumph over adversity. The preacher who listens well to people's feelings will learn to touch upon their hidden or partly told stories in ways that help them to identify with the story of Christian faith and its progress in the world.

Everyone has a story to tell — the child who feels neglected, the housewife who suffers from loneliness and a sense of being unfulfilled, the businesswoman who believes she is passed over for male colleagues with less ability, the student who dreams of doing something to make the whole world notice him, the man who doesn't know how to tell his wife he is having an affair, even the theologian who is trying to make sense of his or her career in the light of an ancient gospel. As Frederick Buechner has written: "At its heart most theology, like most fiction, is essentially autobiography. Aquinas, Calvin, Barth, Tillich, working out their systems in their own ways and in their own language, are all telling us the stories of their lives, and if you press them far enough, even at their most cerebral and forbidding, you find an experience of flesh and blood, a human face smiling or frowning or weeping or covering its eyes before something that happened once."[12]

What the preacher does, when he or she is being effective, is to lay hold of the individual's story and relate it to *the* story, the good news and history of the faith, in such a way that the individual discovers new resources for solving problems, renewing life, or enjoying the world, and in turn contributes to the ongoing story of faith. The sermon in which this is done may itself be an extended story or it may contain shorter stories as illustrations or it may be merely an exposition of a problem or a situation that has story qualities because it applies so obviously to the life stories of people in the congregation. What makes it storypreaching is its sensitivity to the basic needs and desires of people's everyday humanity and its capacity for gaining a hearing through the use of convincing details or verisimilitude.

It is at this point that the preacher's own humanity becomes most important to preaching, for it is often from our knowledge of ourselves and our innermost feelings that we are able to develop for others the true meaning of the gospel in daily affairs. It was once a standard caveat of professors of homiletics that preachers should never allude to themselves or their personal beliefs when instructing others in matters of faith. Now we realize that this was a misguided emphasis and that it denied the very principle of incarnation in Christianity. The preacher's story is important too, especially as it serves the prismatic function of catching the gospel's rays and refracting them into the particular situations of others' lives.

What the preacher must beware of is telling stories about himself or herself that place the preacher in a favorable light. Then the stories appear to be self-serving and often work to undermine people's confidence in the preacher's message. But any story or allusion that represents the preacher in an awkward or failing or fully human light is potentially helpful to the cause of the sermon, which is to enable people to see the application of the good news of Christ to the variable particularities of human existence.

John R. Claypool has given a striking example of this in *The Preaching Event*. When he was minister at Crescent Hill Baptist Church in Louisville, his ten-year-old daughter died of leukemia. For a month Claypool did not reenter the pulpit. When he did go back, he poured out to the congregation his deepest feelings, including his bewilderment and his anger with God. A few people, who expected the preacher to bound back into the pulpit with nothing but classic affirmations, were chagrined at Claypool's expression of humanity; but the majority seemed to feel a new kinship to him. The experience led him to write: "Perhaps our greatest usefulness to each other is not in the relation of strength to weakness — the stance of a rescuer — but in that of weakness to weakness — the two of us in the darkness together, but for that reason no longer alone or without hope."[13]

The preacher who speaks confessionally, in other words, is not holding up self as a model of righteous behavior, but holding up life as an enigma and trying, with the congregation, to see God through it. Thus the congregation is trained to see life as a story intersecting with *the* story and is sent away with new eyes for seeing the many places where the two stories converge upon each other.

THE VALUE OF PSYCHOLOGY

The preacher who is eager to make sermons truly responsive to human need would do well to study psychology and personality theory. The greatest preachers of earlier ages have been ardent students of human nature and so have arrived at valuable insights about life even without the aid of classes in psychology. But the years since Freud have been so productive of important behavioral studies that any minister, even one relatively young and inexperienced, can now understand more about the patterns of human response and development than most ministers formerly knew in a lifetime.

Books by Adler, Jung, Horney, Piaget, Erikson, Bowlby, Maslow, Bettelheim, Bronfenbrenner, and other psychiatrists and psychologists should be on our shelves beside volumes by Barth, Tillich, Bonhoeffer, and Von Rad. They will help us not only to recognize our people within their pages but to preach with a larger knowledge of the episodic character of human life and of the broader outlines of the anxieties, neuroses, and problems that affect us all.

Consider, for example, the helpful studies of recent years on the stages of adult development. Years ago Erik Erikson sketched the general periods of adult life and labeled them according to the psychological "work" to be done by persons passing through them. Then Gail Sheehy, a reporter, did extensive research on these periods and published an enormously popular book called *Passages: The Predictable Crises of Adult Life*. This book was soon followed by Daniel Levinson's important work entitled *The Seasons of a Man's Life*. Levinson's research, done in the lives of forty men over a period of several years, demonstrated that all men go through definable rhythms of change and stability in their career lives and that these rhythms can be charted roughly according to the men's ages. There are stress-filled transition periods around the ages of thirty, forty, fifty, and sixty, when most men experience psychological upheaval and the need for readjustment. Those who elude upheaval in one or more of these crisis times will probably compensate for it with a more difficult transition period at another of the stages. Now there are numerous books dealing with rhythmic crises in people's lives, and Prof. James W. Fowler of Emory University has published a significant treatise called *Stages of Faith* that applies the insights of life periodicity to the development of personal faith.

The kind of information contained in these and other developmental studies is of great advantage to the preacher. It not only helps the preacher to cope with his or her own predictable crises but enables the preacher to plan sermons that anticipate developmental problems in many lives in the congregation, thus providing significant support from the structures of biblical faith and theology.

After John Claypool discovered the importance of confessional preaching, for instance, he joined the reading of Sheehy's *Passages* to his personal experiences and produced a sermon series that had an electrifying effect upon his Fort Worth congregation. Called *Stages: The Art of Living the Expected*,[14] the series focused on four episodes in the life of the biblical character David, showing him in critical moments of childhood, adolescence, adulthood, and senior adulthood. The Davidic material became a framework for exploring the meaning of these stages for all of us. Members of the congregation found the series helpful in understanding not only their own situations but those of parents, children, friends, and other persons with whom they had significant relationships. They also learned how the gospel is related to the entire cycle of human life, not only to the moment of initiation or conversion.

For many persons in our congregations, the insights of psychology are fresh and exciting in themselves and will prove helpful to them in understanding their general human situations. For those who have read more widely in popular psychology, the linking of psychology and theology will contribute to valuable new understandings of the place of faith in everyday living. Instead of experiencing psychology as merely another humanistic discipline challenging the authority of God in the world, they will find it helpful for the kind of self-analysis that leads to an actual recovery of the sense of God's presence in their lives.

THE "PLUS" IN THE MIXTURE

It is important, of course, that the sermon not be turned into a mere lecture on human psychology. We are called to be preachers of the gospel, not professors of mental hygiene. The insights of psychology can illumine many dark and shadowy places in our understanding, but they should not be confused with the Light who has come into the world for the redemption of all people.

Faithful preachers keep the humanistic disciplines and biblical theology in creative tension with one another and use psychological understanding to explore more fully the meaning of the gospel in the modern world. The sword, of course, cuts both ways: while biblical faith may sometimes insist on principles that counter the normatizing tendencies of psychological studies, psychology also acts critically upon certain biblical passages and concepts. For example, current psychology strongly supports the feminist position against the apparent maleism of early Christian leaders, especially the apostle Paul, and insists on a less fundamentalist approach to sexuality in contemporary Christianity. Ministers today must study diligently, reflect deeply, and make their commitments in such matters on an ad hoc basis, cautiously but courageously following their insights. The important thing is that the major biblical parameters of love, faith, community, life in Christ, and the sovereignty of God continue to be the mainstays of our preaching, providing the overall form to be illuminated by the studies of psychologists and psychiatrists.

The basic thrust of any sermon depends largely on the personal faith of the preacher, for sermons are only momentary extrusions from the internal life and experience of the persons delivering them. They reflect the status within, points in a personal journey. If the preacher is faithful in his or her devotional life, this will shine through in the various parts of the sermon without having to be spotlighted. A Christlike mood or spirit will prevail: an aura of biblical faith will subtly alter everything in the sermon.

"Some ideas and attitudes can be implicit in a sermon," says Edgar Jackson. "Not every sermon can be about faith, but every sermon can breathe a sense of faith. Not every message can be on the value of the human soul, but every sermon should assume it. Not every homily can deal with problem-solving techniques, but every sermon can assume the presence of a power able to help solve the most serious of human difficulties. Nor can every sermon be theological, but neither should any sermon give a basis for doubt as to the preacher's feeling that God is a real and present force in life."[15]

It is a good idea, however, to survey one's sermons occasionally to see which ideas and attitudes are *explicit* in them. Some persons in our congregations are less sensitive to spiritual qualities than others and need simple, directly stated truths to be their guiding lights for daily living. The brightest preachers often forget this. Their own preference for subtlety leads them to preach intelligent, carefully shaded sermons that are aesthetically satisfying to the keener minds in their congregations, while other minds fail to see their points and thus are left without ample guidance from the pulpit. Preachers with doubts about the clarity of their ideas expressed from the pulpit would do well to study the sermons of Clovis Chappell and J. Wallace Hamilton, whose great popular followings were directly related to the simplicity of their presentations. These preachers were simple but never shallow. Hamilton especially was a vigorous reader of psychology and often cited Freud, Jung, and Adler in his sermons. But there was never any doubt, when he had finished preaching, that it was Jesus and not Freud who had been exalted.

We must beware of becoming mere "pop" psychologists, using the data or insights of psychology to get our sermons started and then abandoning them without any interest in working through them for the congregation. We will be tempted to do this, for it makes us seem "hip" or knowledgeable, especially among college students and young adults in the congregation, without costing us much in terms of a genuine dialogue between psychology and theology. But such a practice soon undermines confidence in our thinking and puts the gospel in a bad light, with the inference that it cannot stand up to a full confrontation with modern science.

In *Pastor, Preacher, Person*, David Switzer has written wisely on this matter. "The preacher," he says, "must beware of the particular style of presumed 'preaching to meet people's needs' which picks up on a particular problem area, labels it, and then gives some 'Christian' answers to it. When such an approach slides over into an easy, palliative, 'inspirational' sermon, it often does not communicate to persons the depth and complexity and conflicting nature of human emotions and experiences which comprise the reality of their lives, and even though some may 'like' the sermon, it does not lead them into the experience of being understood, and thereby not into the difficult process of self-exploration which is the prior and essential condition for effective decision-making and change."[16]

Switzer does not condemn psychological preaching in general, but the form of it that uses psychology only as a gimmick or hook for introducing the gospel. His remarks occur in the context of a plea for preachers really to listen to the persons in their congregations and to couch their sermons in empathic language that accurately reflects where the people are and what they are feeling. If preachers understand themselves and listen to their congregations, they will not make cheap, irresponsible use of psychological insights and information.

Elsewhere in his book Switzer discusses the similarity between the preaching process and the counseling process. In both processes, he says, the aim is to lead people from *self-exploration* to *goal setting* to *evaluation of alternatives* to *decision making* to *action* to *self-exploration* again, and so on.[17]

Progress in the individual's life is thus viewed spirally, not linearly. By implication, what Switzer says about irresponsible psychological preaching can be interpreted as applying to preaching that does not lead persons in the congregation through all of these stages. That is, it might be preaching that promotes self-exploration by raising certain psychological questions but does not carry persons on to the stage of goal setting; or it might take them through self-evaluation and goal setting but stop short of considering alternatives; or it might conceivably fulfill all the criteria but fail to lead from action to more self-exploration.

THE EXAMPLE OF FOSDICK

What Switzer says seems very demanding. We wonder whether we can really measure up to such a requirement for preaching. In fact, we wonder whether anyone could.

But it is really less impossible than it seems.

The preaching of Harry Emerson Fosdick is an illustration. Fosdick's study of the sermons of F. W. Robertson, Henry Ward Beecher, and Phillips Brooks, three of the greatest nineteenth-century preachers, convinced him that the most effective preaching is always directed to individuals, not merely to congregations in general. From his counseling experience, he learned that individuals are rarely interested in general theses from the Bible or theology but are invariably concerned about specific human problems. It was a simple step to the conclusion that people would respond most readily to sermons dealing with particular problems treated in the light of biblical or theological truth.

Basically Fosdick attempted to do four things in each sermon: (1) To identify a pressing human problem and gain each hearer's personal interest in it. (2) To develop understanding of the problem in terms of common solutions people have tried, usually without success. (3) To set the problem in the biblical perspective and secure the hearer's cooperation in discovering how much richer and more satisfying that perspective is than any other. (4) To encourage the hearer to accept and act on the biblical answer to his or her problem, thus mastering the problem and preparing to meet life at a higher level.

It is easy to correlate these efforts with the requirements laid upon sermons by Switzer. Identifying the problem and securing the listener's interest corresponds to *self-exploration* and *goal setting* (assuming that the goal is to solve the problem). Studying the world's answers to the problem is the *evaluation of alternatives.* Setting the problem in the perspective of biblical faith also belongs to the evaluation of alternatives, but begins to move the hearer past that to the *decision-making* stage. The encouragement to accept and act on the biblical way leads to *action* and, it is hoped, to further reflection or *self-exploration* at the new level of existence.

Suppose we examine a specific sermon by Fosdick to see how he set about solving an important human problem. We will consider one called "Making the Best of a Bad Mess," which was preached during the early years of the Great Depression and again, with alterations, during the dark years of World War II. The text is Titus 1:5, "For this cause left I thee in Crete, that thou shouldest set in order the things that are wanting, and ordain elders in every city, as I had appointed thee" (KJV).

Fosdick began the sermon, contrary to his usual practice of describing or illustrating some modern problem, with reference to the text itself; only he did it so imaginatively that it immediately came to grips with the modern situation. He imagined for his congregation the letter that Titus must have sent to Paul to provoke this one from Paul. In it Titus complained to Paul about the terrible place to which Paul had assigned him. The Cretans, he said, were "an awful lot"—liars, thieves, cheats, and murderers. He wanted to get out of there, and the sooner, the better.

Paul replied with the letter we have. His answer was understanding, but firm. If Crete had not been a bad place, there would have been no reason to send Titus there. "For this cause," said Paul, "left I thee in Crete." The phrase is repeated several times in the introduction to the sermon, each time with great solemnity. It echoes throughout the sermon. "For this cause left I thee in Crete." No one who heard the sermon could possibly have forgotten it. It made—and still makes—an indelible impression.

Fosdick offered three primary observations in the sermon, all of which are aspects of a single point, that sometimes we must make the best of a bad mess. First, happiness is not something you find, it is something you create. Titus had to discover his happiness in Crete and we have to discover ours in the midst of difficulties too. Second, we can't pretend to be disciples of Jesus if we are unwilling to stay in Crete, because Jesus belongs in Crete; the whole message of the incarnation is that he came to Crete to die for our sins. And third, the ultimate test of our faith is its power not to deliver us from the hard places of life but to see us through them.

There is no namby-pamby, peace-of-mind Christianity in this sermon. It says very flatly that there are times in life when there is no honorable or Christlike way to retreat from hard and undesirable situations; instead, we have to stick them out and turn difficulty into victory by following Christ, who died on a cross. The sermon is packed with illustrations of persons who faced hardships and overcame them with courage, loyalty, and imagination. In almost every one of these illustrations can be seen the alternatives Fosdick's listeners were given to ponder: running away, selling out, giving up, breaking down, asking for easier assignments. But the biblical answer, the only triumphant alternative, was the one seen in Christ and the apostles — to stay in Crete and turn it into the kind of situation they dreamed of being in.

The final illustration of the sermon was a sentimental one involving a small boy who was having nightmares in which he was attacked by a tiger. The boy was taken to a psychiatrist. The psychiatrist told him he must make friends with the tiger. The next time he had the nightmare, he was to reach out his hand and say, "Hello, old fellow," and convert him into an ally. The boy did it; bravely, when the tiger appeared again, he thrust out his hand and said, "Hello, old fellow"— and the implication is that he was never again troubled by the tiger.

Even if sentimental, the story had a certain power after the cumulative effect of the sermon. And it is a clear indication of Fosdick's eagerness to take the final step in the cycle of progression described by Switzer, of helping his listeners to move from *decision making* to *action*. People were given a very concrete picture of the way they could behave toward whatever problems were menacing their lives; they could extend their hands, say "Hello, old fellow," and make the best of a bad mess.

We can only imagine the kinds of people who heard the sermon when it was preached at Riverside: businessmen wiped out by the crash; housewives living in intolerable home situations; university professors whose colleges could not afford to pay their salaries; diplomats who saw no hope for the world; old people whose children no longer wanted them; young people whose parents had turned them out; even ministers whose congregations could no longer pay them. The air must have been charged with the electricity of their thoughts and feelings.

The situation is not that different for any of us when we preach today. There are still as many problems as there are people. The gospel is still full of resolution and challenge. We only have to find the will and the imagination to get the two things together—the problems and the gospel—and to preach our sermons in a manner that will help people to work through from one to the other. Then they too can shake hands with their tigers.

NOTES

1. Phillips Brooks, *Eight Lectures on Preaching* (London: S.P.C.K., 1959), p. 77.

2. Henri J. M. Nouwen, *Creative Ministry* (New York: Doubleday & Co., Image Books, 1978), p. 25.

3. William H. Willimon, *Worship as Pastoral Care* (Nashville: Abingdon Press, 1979).

4. David H. C. Read, *The Communication of the Gospel* (London: SCM Press, 1952), p. 62.

5. Edgar Jackson, *How to Preach to People's Needs* (Nashville: Abingdon Press, 1956), p. 14.

6. Percy Bysshe Shelley, "A Defense of Poetry," in *Anthology of Romanticism*, ed. Ernest Bernbaum (New York: Ronald Press, 1948), p. 979.

7. Fred Craddock, *As One Without Authority* (Enid, Okla.: Phillips University Press, 1971), pp. 51–76.

8. Reuel L. Howe, *Partners in Preaching: Clergy and Laity in Dialogue* (New York: Seabury Press, 1967), p. 85.

9. Harry Emerson Fosdick, "What Is the Matter with Preaching?" in *Harry Emerson Fosdick's Art of Preaching: An Anthology*, ed. Lionel Crocker (Springfield, Ill.: Charles C. Thomas, 1971), p. 28.

10. Ibid., p. 29.

11. Bruno Bettelheim, *The Uses of Enchantment* (London: Thames and Hudson, 1976).

12. Frederick Buechner, *The Alphabet of Grace* (New York: Seabury Press, 1970), p. 3.

13. John R. Claypool, *The Preaching Event* (Waco, Tex.: Word Books, 1980), p. 107.

14. John R. Claypool, *Stages: The Art of Living the Expected* (Waco, Tex.: Word Books, 1977).

15. Jackson, *How to Preach to People's Needs*, pp. 15–16.

16. David K. Switzer, *Pastor, Preacher, Person: Developing a Pastoral Ministry in Depth* (Nashville: Abingdon Press, 1979), pp. 75–76.

17. Ibid., p. 65.

──4──
Constructing the Sermon

Now we arrive at the real test of the preacher's dedication to the task of preaching—whether he or she is willing to pay for the actual shaping of the sermon. It is one thing to entertain glorious dreams of the preaching that one *could* do. But it is quite another thing to be ready to work at it, to carry it in one's thoughts day and night, to tinker with outlines or sermon plans until they are just right, to sweat over the wording until it is both vivid and precise, and, finally, to get it all inside one's head for preaching, the way one gets a firm hold of any important word to be said to people who really matter.

Few preachers possess the brilliance or facility of James Pike, the famous bishop of California who had a disturbingly casual approach to preaching. Pike said he gave some thought to sermon material on Saturday night, consulted a few commentaries, and formed "a kind of outline" in his mind. He reflected on the outline after going to bed and again in the morning. Then he went into the pulpit and preached, usually without any notes at all.[1] Pike was an extraordinary man with a striking personality. Trained as a lawyer, he had an aptness for thinking quickly on his feet. He also knew the advantage of looking people directly in the eye while speaking to them. And he argued that the preacher who does not write out a manuscript of the sermon uses oral language, whereas the one who writes becomes high-flown and difficult to understand.

Great preachers, however, seldom agree with Pike's assessment.

Most of them have worked assiduously at their sermons, the way great novelists work at their novels or great poets at their poetry. W. E. Sangster chose his sermon themes at least ten days in advance and then worked at the sermons every day until they were ready. George Buttrick spent a minimum of twenty-five to thirty hours on each sermon he was to deliver—in most cases, more than an hour per minute for the finished product. Paul Scherer sometimes devoted forty hours to a single sermon.

It is true that some written sermons are turgid and Latinate, but that proves nothing. The same preachers' sermons, when they do not write, may still be turgid and Latinate. The trouble is that they do not know how to write sermons. They have not caught the trick of writing oral language. They have not learned enough about simplicity in outlines, vividness in illustrations, and clarity in expression. Their craft is only half-baked. Instead of rejecting a written sermon for its apparent insufficiency, they should work harder on it, carrying it to the point where it achieves the desired effect.

Nor is it worthwhile to argue, as some do, that careful preparation of sermons inhibits the working of the Holy Spirit. Such an argument intentionally misunderstands the nature of preparation, setting it over against prayer and attentiveness to the voice of the Lord. The truth is, one can pray and listen more conscientiously in the study while working on the sermon than while standing in the pulpit facing a congregation. A spiritually inclined minister waits sensitively before God while reading and studying the Scripture, when choosing a theme and forming an outline, while writing the sermon, and throughout the business of getting hold of the sermon for effective delivery.

The only real despisers of craft are poor craftspersons. Others realize that there is no worthwhile achievement without work and practice. A Picasso may appear to dash off a masterpiece with little or no effort, but the effortlessness merely belies the years of disciplined struggle behind the present moment. A Rubinstein may sit at the piano and play with apparent ease a difficult composition he has never seen before, but he is able to do this because of years of drilling on scales and arpeggios and mastering other difficult pieces. By the same token, a gifted preacher may occasionally rise and deliver an apparently flawless sermon concocted only a few moments before, but the likelihood of his or her doing this increases geometrically in proportion to the number of years the preacher has been conscientiously working at the craft of preaching. If God spent six days making a world, it should be no dishonor to the preacher to spend two or three days making a sermon.

GETTING THE IDEA

The first thing in making a sermon, the sine qua non, is the idea. There can be no sermon that was not first preceded by an idea or a theme. The novelist Henry James called the idea in storywriting the "germ." It is the bacterial beginning, the point of conception, he said, for every work of art or creation. The same is true for the idea of the sermon; it is the germ, the insight, from which eventually the entire sermon is grown.

The idea for the sermon may come in one of two ways. If the preacher follows a lectionary, so that the text for each Sunday's sermon is determined ahead of time, the idea will usually come while he or she is brooding on the Scripture. The preacher's mind will be hovering over the text the way one pictures the Spirit of God hovering over the void at the time of creation; suddenly a single shaft of light will penetrate the murkiness, and that light will become the center of the world — or, in this case, of the sermon. If the preacher does not use a lectionary, the idea may come at any time. Experienced ministers carry a notebook with them to jot down the insights that will become sermons; some even keep a pad by the bedside in case the ideas come at night. They know the preciousness of the commodity and are like the whalers in Melville's *Moby Dick*, who wounded all the whales they could whenever they happened upon a school of them, knowing they could go back later and kill them at their leisure.

Many ministers are unfortunately lazy at this first stage of sermon making. They fail to record the fleeting insights and probably lose 90 percent of the best sermon ideas they ever get. I wish they could know Madeleine L'Engle, the novelist and essayist. Madeleine is an indefatigable note maker. At a conference, she is

44

at the breakfast table before anyone else, using the time to set down observations, reflections, and new ideas in her journal. At night, when others are having a good time singing and visiting, she scribbles away in her book, sequestering the thoughts that will become the basis for future writings. Her journal keeps her, she says, and she must keep her journal.

Ernest Campbell, who was for several years minister of Riverside Church in New York, keeps a small pocket notebook with him at all times and can be seen making entries in it while riding a bus, reading a book, or chatting with friends at lunch. When he has filled one of these small books, he tosses it into a desk drawer that is half filled with similar books. From time to time he spends an hour or two thumbing through the books and perusing the notes. Invariably several notes spring forth, ripe for further development. They become the germs of upcoming sermons.

What do the notes in a preacher's notebooks look like? Here are random examples from my own book. They are sketchy and in the original contained numerous abbreviations. Some were prompted by reading Scripture, some by reading other books. Some merely happened.

"Jesus and the Terror of Moving." Woman who approached me at conference in Indianapolis to talk about her husband's taking job in another city; she was terrified at leaving her home, her friends, the familiar city. What does the gospel say to her? Include John R. Mott's card, which said: "With Christ, anywhere in the world; without him, not even across the threshold."

From Sam Keen's *Beginning Without End*. Speaking of his broken life. Says the future does not grow out of the past but out of the DEATH of the past. Sermon on "Except a grain of wheat fall in the ground and die . . ."?

Sermon title: HURRY UP AND SLOW DOWN. On meditation and Christian life. Maybe Christian action.

Annie Dillard, *Pilgrim at Tinker Creek*, p. 81: "You catch grace as a man fills his cup under a waterfall." Sermon on THE CUP AND THE WATERFALL.

Sermon title: ARE YOU GIVING ANY CHRISTMAS PRESENCE THIS YEAR? On keeping Christmas in meaningful ways.

Maybe use text of the Magi, who came and *adored* — didn't just bring gifts.

Sermon intro: The bright wonder of seed catalogs that come on gloomy winter days. How I pore over them — luscious raspberries and strawberries, jonquils and azaleas, etc. Cf. Paul's passage on Christ as "firstfruits" — as promise in the dark days of this life. Possible title: SOMETHING BRIGHT FOR A DULL DAY. Maybe also the moral: If I don't do something about the garden now, there won't be any raspberries and strawberries next summer.

You see how it works. Enough must be entered into the notebook to recall the entire idea, but it is best not to attempt to be too comprehensive. I find that expanding a note very much does something to kill its magic for me when I go back to glance over my notebook.

W. E. Sangster, on the other hand, always placed each idea at the head of a fresh page in his notebook so that he could enter future reflections beneath it. He then "tended" his notebooks by reading through them, adding reflections as they occurred to him, and waiting until particular items were ready to be used. The wealth of his notebooks always assured him of the sermons he needed. "I have never been in the state of mind," he said, "of wondering what to say. Subjects always seem abundant. Indeed, they jostle each other in my mind and elbow their way to the front. As I turn over the pages of my notebook they seem to say: 'My turn next.'"[2]

REFINING THE IDEA

Aside from the convenience of a notebook full of ideas, there is another good reason for storing one's thoughts in this manner. Ideas as they first occur to the preacher may not be in their final, most preachable form. They need to season — to ripen — before being used.

Ideas have a seductive power, especially over persons not accustomed to having many of them, and we are inclined to use them improperly, so that we don't take full advantage of them. Many novelists and playwrights let their best ideas season for a while before acting on them. So do architects, scientists, and business entrepreneurs. That way they have the upper hand over the ideas, and not vice versa. Similarly the preacher who waits for a few weeks, or even a few days, before acting on an exciting new sermon idea often judges the idea better than when it occurred, seeing both its possibilities and its limitations with a more critical eye.

For example, if I had rushed ahead to compose a sermon when I first thought of the connection between seed catalogs on a winter's day and Paul's description of Christ as "the firstfruits of them that slept," I would probably have preached a doctrinal sermon on the resurrection. The sermon would most likely have begun with the idea about the seed catalogs, moved to the Pauline material, and accomplished little more than communicating the idea itself. Now, reflecting on the idea after it has lain in my notebook for months, I am more prepared to subordinate the idea to other possibilities. I might begin the sermon not with this idea but with a reference to people's depression in the routines of life, a depression which, for Christians, should be dispelled by awareness of the presence of Christ. Then, in the course of the sermon, the idea about the seed catalog would become an illustration of the way recalling the resurrection can brighten one's outlook, rescuing it from the doldrums it falls upon. The difference in the two approaches may appear slight; yet the second method has the *people* at its center, not the idea, and that is a vital distinction. The first way would have exhibited the cleverness of the idea; the second subordinates cleverness to getting something done.

STATING THE PURPOSE OF THE SERMON

At this point, when the idea has seasoned and is ready to be turned into a sermon, it is time to take one of the most important steps in the entire sermon-making process, that of identifying the overall purpose of the sermon. The purpose is not always self-evident in the idea. It may actually lie outside the idea, even though the idea has prompted it. In the example about the seed catalog, the purpose metamorphosed from what it would have been had the idea been employed at once—perhaps, "To illustrate how the resurrection brightens our dark days"—to one centering on the congregation, "To help people deal with their dark days in the light of the resurrection." The initial idea itself is merely reflected in the final statement of purpose; it is not actually there.

Sermons often flounder because their preachers have not identified their purpose before beginning them. They are like the Eskimo's sled with the huskies tied all around it instead of in a straight rein in front: their direction is uncertain. The ingredients of a good sermon may be present—a spiritual attitude, clever ideas, good language, illuminative analogies or illustrations—so that both the preacher and the congregation are puzzled about why nothing seems to *happen* in the sermon. But without a clear purpose in mind the preacher cannot hope to accomplish much. As James D. Glasse once remarked, "If we do not know where we are going, we will not know when we get there."

This is the first benefit of a well-stated purpose: it identifies the thrust of the sermon. It locates from the outset the lines of force in the message. Then everything else in the sermon can be subordinated to these lines. Points and ideas can be brought into subjugation. Illustrations that tend to mislead or distract from the primary thrust can be rejected in favor of others. The overall design of the sermon can be orchestrated in a way that will serve the purpose from beginning to end. Then no one will go home from church wondering what the sermon was about; the direction will be clear to preacher and people alike.

There is a second benefit to early identification of the sermon's purpose: it permits the preacher to assess the worthiness of the purpose and, if necessary, to adjust the purpose before proceeding to the outline and the composition of the sermon. It is a disappointing experience to expend the effort to write a sermon and then to feel that it is not worth preaching. The preacher may avoid this impasse by taking a hard look at the purpose before undertaking the actual work on the sermon. After explicitly stating the purpose, the preacher can ask: Is this a theme to justify my work and the people's time? Will it serve an important purpose in the congregation? Can I improve it in any way in order to sharpen the focus of the sermon?

"No sermon," said John Henry Jowett, "is ready for preaching, nor ready for writing out, until we can express its theme in a short, pregnant sentence as clear as crystal. I find the getting of that sentence is the hardest, the most exacting, and the most fruitful labor in my study."[3]

Sangster expressed the same sense of urgency about the statement of purpose. Key words suggest that he may have had Jowett's remarks in mind when he wrote:

> Thoughts flood in. I note the good ones. If they are a little slow in coming at first, they are soon too numerous: they have to be brought under the discipline of one idea — one ruling phrase. Finding that phrase is often the hardest work. Over and over in my mind the subject goes. One cannot preach *all* grace, or *all* mercy, or *all* punishment in one sermon. What is the *aspect* I must deal with here? How can I de-limit the theme? If the sermon is to have wholeness and tautness, I must have a single high and clear aim. Is it this? . . . Is it that? . . . No! IT IS THIS! I have it! Down it goes at the top of another blank sheet of paper. *That is it!* I will say *that.* God's imprimatur is on it. I felt the warm assurance in my heart as it flashed on my mind. What a theme! I will hold that up, God helping me, in all the sovereignty of truth, and the Holy Spirit will own it and God will do His work.

"With the aspect of the subject decided and clearly expressed in one pregnant phrase," concludes Sangster, "I turn my mind to the structure of the sermon."[4]

Sometimes it helps to clarify the theme or purpose if one asks a question such as: What am I trying to do to these people? What do I wish them to see? What would I like to have happen in their minds as I preach? The answer to any of these questions should be forthcoming in a simple, clear phrase.

The statement of purpose is rarely the same thing as the idea or the illustration that initiated the sermon. Nor is it always the same as the theological point expressed by the scriptural text. Often it will be at least slightly different from the thrust of the text. Mark

6:45–52, for example, is the account of Jesus' walking on the water at night, getting into the boat with the disciples, and calming the troubled sea. In its context, it is about the power of Christ and the slowness of the disciples to understand—a constant theme in Mark. A sermon on the text, however, might well have as its central purpose *to remind people whose lives are troubled that Christ still comes to us with the power to restore order and tranquillity.* The original thrust of the text is retained, but is redirected toward the people who are at the center of the preaching focus.

Arriving at this clear, succinct statement of purpose, as Jowett said, is not always easy. Often we wrestle with a text and several ideas before we are able to clarify in our minds what it is we really desire to do in the sermon. But once we have identified the purpose, the sermon is well under way. We have an organizing principle for dealing with all our material. Like a magnet enforcing order on a random arrangement of iron filings, the statement of purpose will produce the alignments necessary for constructing a sound, helpful sermon.

VARIETIES OF STRUCTURE

Now we are at the point of deciding what kind of form the sermon shall take. Most preachers adapt a single form to their purposes and use it with only slight variations for the remainder of their ministries. But there are many styles and varieties of homiletical form, and a creative preacher, while hewing primarily to one form, will occasionally try other forms, if only to enhance the communication process. Periodic experimentation offers freshness and variety to the people who listen to our sermons week after week and, in addition to giving us new perspectives on the material we are preaching, permits us to make value judgments about the forms and methods we ordinarily employ.

The work of poets is instructive: they constantly experiment with verse forms as part of the urging of their craft. For weeks they will work at sonnets, trying to imitate the magic of Shakespeare or Elizabeth Barrett Browning or Gerard Manley Hopkins; then they will try odes and see if they can evoke the spirit of Shelley;

then they will turn to longer, more narrative poetry in the style of Eliot or Yeats, and so on. If Marshall McLuhan was right, that "the medium is the message," or if he was only partly right and the medium *affects* the message, then preachers have an obligation to shift styles from time to time in order to hear their own voices in new ways and to discover the impact that different forms will have on the message they attempt to preach.

There have been so many forms for the sermon through the centuries that it would be impossible to catalog all of them here or even to discuss all of those presently in service. But we can at least note in a general way several of the more important forms employed in recent times. They are (1) the impressionistic sermon, (2) the developmental sermon, (3) the expository sermon, (4) the classification sermon, (5) the faceting sermon, and (6) the experimental sermon.

1. *The impressionistic sermon.* It is almost anomalous to call this a sermon form, for it is one of the most formless of sermons, consisting primarily of the minister's casual remarks, offered with little attempt at structure. In art the form would be analogous to an artist's sketch as opposed to a painting or drawing in which the artist had worked for fullness and detail. In music it would be equivalent to a simple tune or ditty as opposed to a fully orchestrated composition. Seeking freedom from conventional restraints, the minister simply prepares a few sentences or paragraphs on a theme, idea, or impression and offers these as the sermon at the appointed time in the liturgy.

Many preachers adopted this style of preaching in the 1960s and 1970s, contending that it is a more natural way to preach and therefore more acceptable than traditional sermons in our freedom-conscious era. Others are convinced that it is more spiritual than are conventional forms because it does not interpose considerations of style between prayerful reflection and the act of preaching to a congregation. And still others have supported it because, of all the forms of preaching, it is probably least costly to the preacher in terms of time spent in preparation.

The reader who wishes to examine some impressionistic sermons that are extremely well done and probably did cost their author some time and energy in preparation is directed to the preaching of John Fry, who was minister of First Presbyterian Church of Chicago during the late 1960s.[5] Fry's sermons are not as brief as impressionistic sermons often are; they are, in fact, rather conventional in length. But they proceed with a casual manner, without apparent organization, and are therefore difficult to reproduce in summary form. Fry was taught in seminary to outline sermons in a more classical way, but he no longer believes in outlines. Classical preaching, he says, is anachronistic now, as out of place in an ordinary congregation as "a Lyceum lecture at a go-go palace or a Klan rally."[6]

Some preachers are easily convinced by such an argument, for they wish to avoid the stuffiness and formality of much of the preaching they have heard. But the inexperienced preacher should be warned that the impressionistic sermon is not as easy to do well as one might expect. Snappy and attractive the first time or two around (people will probably say, "I liked that, it was down to earth and to the point"), it soon wears thin and congregations are likely to complain that it is simply not as nourishing and helpful as more conventional sermons. The wise pastor will probably experiment with it occasionally and try, if he or she finds it pleasurable to use, to moderate between it and the next form of the sermon — developmental preaching.

2. *The developmental sermon.* The developmental sermon is the one that has a central idea or controlling purpose that is worked out through a series of two or more progressive stages in which the idea or purpose grows to its climax. It is the workhorse form of the Christian pulpit, the one most frequently taught in seminaries and used on Sunday morning. It is the contemporary version of the classical form decried by John Fry. Fry is both right and wrong. He is right about sermons that have a nineteenth-century odor about them. He is wrong about the ones that don't. And that odor is not, as he assumes, the product of form; it is instead the product of a certain frame of mind, a way of thinking that tends to produce, along with the nineteenth-century method of structuring a sermon, the theological and rhetorical emphases

of the nineteenth century. The two things, structure and tone, do not have to go together. Many skillful preachers today use the developmental sermon without sounding at all old-fashioned. They simply develop their points more quickly than preachers once did, using fresh imagery and illustrations, and address themselves to the contemporary congregation.

The reason the classical sermon form—an introduction, two, three, or four points, and a deft conclusion—has endured from the nineteenth century into the present is the same reason it endured from the Middle Ages to the Reformation to the time of Wesley and Whitefield—it is an eminently serviceable way of preparing and communicating a message. It has undergone subtle changes from one era to the next, mostly in terms of simplification. But it has remained the basic method of sermon preparation through the ages because experience has shown that it works effectively.

Every student of preaching ought to master this form, just as every artist ought in the beginning to master the use of basic art forms. Then if he or she wishes to depart from this use by simplifying it in the direction of the impressionistic sermon or by adopting totally different forms, the departure will be a matter of real freedom and not of necessity because the preacher could not manage the traditional form. Once accustomed to this method, however, most preachers make it their staple homiletical form, abandoning it only infrequently for the sake of variety or because a particular theme demands a different treatment. They sense the power, solidity, and dependability of the form and feel good about its use from week to week.

3. *The expository sermon.* This form of preaching, as the name implies, consists of giving exposition or running commentary on the biblical text. Once a rather popular variety of preaching, especially in the more traditional and conservative churches, the expository sermon is less frequently employed today, possibly because a generation of biblically sensitive preachers is more aware of the dangers of eisegesis, or reading unwarranted meanings into the words and phrases of Scripture.

Clovis Chappell, who pastored large Methodist churches in Washington, Houston, Memphis, Birmingham, and Charlotte, was a great expository preacher who had a facility for making passages and situations in the Bible come alive for the congregation. His sermon "A Glimpse of the After Life," for example, is an unforgettable reexamination of Luke 16:19–31, the story of the rich man and Lazarus. Here is a paragraph exemplifying Chappell's style:

> "There was a certain rich man" — what is the meaning of the word? Rich man — it stands for power, capacity, ability to serve. "And there was a beggar that lay at his gate full of sores" — that means need. And so we have here ability to serve and a need of service brought close together. The poor man was at the rich man's gate. That means that this poor man was the rich man's responsibility. He was the rich man's opportunity. I do not know what responsibility lay at the gate of the man across the street, but the responsibility of this rich man is very plain. The call for help is loud and insistent. Here was his chance. Here was his opportunity. Here was the safety vault in which he might have made a deposit for eternity.[7]

The great advantage of this form of preaching lies in the way its hearers are taught from the Bible. There is great ignorance of the Bible in our time, and frequent use of the expository method can help to offset this. One of the often recurring words in expository sermons is the verb "to mean." "This *means* . . ." "That *means* . . ." We encounter it again and again in Chappell or in anyone who employs the form. It underlines the teaching significance of the method.

But the novice should be warned that exposition is also a very difficult method to master. It appears simple, but is not. It requires first an accurate knowledge of the text, to be acquired by careful study and exegesis. Then it requires an ample knowledge of human nature and life experience so that the exposition may be directed toward meaningful ends in the hearers and not merely toward the conclusion that the speaker is a knowledgeable person. And finally it requires — or so it is used by the greatest practitioners of the method — a sense of dramatic or psychological order so that the sermon, while still textual in nature, arrives at a suitable climax and conclusion, as if it were a developmental sermon and not an expository one.

4. *The classification sermon.* "There are two types of persons in the world," it has been said, "those who divide the world into two types of persons and those who do not." Some preachers have a penchant for dividing or categorizing themes and ideas. They like to treat a text according to what it says to young persons, to middle-aged persons, and to older persons. They tend to examine a story such as the one about the rich ruler who came to Jesus as it might be perceived by the poor, by the moderately well off, and by the rich. They think of a particular message as it applies to the church, to the community beyond the church, and to the world beyond that.

There is admittedly a kind of orderliness about such classifications. They are neat in the way a pigeonhole desk is neat — a place for everything and everything in its place. But the cumulative power of classification sermons is often extremely limited. Their inner development tends to be impersonal, or at least does not permit the kind of incremental personal involvement encouraged by other forms. Proceeding in a merely logical or didactic sequence (from "young persons" to "middle-aged persons" to "older persons" or from "poor" to "moderately well off" to "rich"), the classification sermon abandons or stands in jeopardy of abandoning any sense of intimacy or involvement it has managed to win in the preceding category. The youth who has been hooked by the sermon during the "young persons" segment begins to lose interest when the preacher moves into the segment about "middle-aged persons." The difference between developmental sermons and classification sermons, in other words, is that in the former preachers move into succeeding gears, while in the latter they move into succeeding rooms.

The classification sermon, because it is easy to use, is also highly addictive. Once a preacher gets the hang of it, he or she is prone to overuse it. Therefore we should be highly conscious of our use of it and try not to employ it more than occasionally. If we do utilize it frequently, our preaching will become highly predictable and people will find it unexciting.

5. *The faceting sermon.* The name of this sermon form was

originated by W. E. Sangster, who borrowed it from the lapidary. Faceting is what jewelers do to precious stones after the stones have been split: they cut faces on the stones so that their beauty may be more easily seen. Before a gem is faceted, it is rough and unattractive; the beauty is imprisoned. But as the jeweler cuts and polishes, dimensions of the beauty begin to leap out of prison, first on one side, then on another, and so on, until the entire gem flashes and shines with the qualities that make rare stones so desirable and expensive.

It is the same with the faceting sermon. The preacher begins by splitting open some great truth, cleaving it the way one would cleave a diamond in the rough. Then, when one enormous facet of the truth has been revealed, the preacher sets to work around that truth, polishing side effects or facets of it until the whole sermon sparkles like a jewel, with every angle irradiating the great truth first introduced.

Phillips Brooks was especially fond of this method. He often exposed a major truth or insight at the beginning of his sermon, then spent the remainder of his time studying the truth from various angles. For example, he preached a sermon called "Standing Before God"[8] on the text "And I saw the dead, small and great, stand before God" (Rev. 20:12). The introduction speaks of the human longing to know what lies beyond death and tells that John, the author of Revelation, had a glimpse of it. The main point, the central facet of the jewel, is that we shall all stand before God in the company of those John beheld and shall be judged by that Presence as a child's being is judged by its father, as an artist's being is judged by beauty, or as a scholar's being is judged by the truth. Having established this point, Brooks proceeds to circumnavigate it, adding to it the following facets:

- When we stand before God the question of rightness becomes preeminent over all other matters, including comfort, popularity, and profit.
- As John saw the dead, great and small, standing before God, we shall all stand on the same level after death, regardless of past distinctions.

- As all generations were seen standing together, we have a picture of the infinite nature of God that is able to hold together the people of all the ages.
- John saw the place to which souls go. We see only the place from which they go. It would help if we could see what he saw.
- We do not need to be dead to stand before God; the wonderful experience of seeing God can begin now.

The fifth facet actually serves as Brooks's conclusion. As we can see, all the points relate to the first point, or primary facet, instead of relating successively to one another. Therefore the conclusion cannot really continue a particular thrust, but must move on to some new consideration.

The faceting sermon is an excellent teaching sermon, for it makes one essential point and then reinforces it in several ways. It reminds one of Stephen Leacock's admonition to himself about the best way to teach: "Take a small bite and chew it well." One danger is that it will not sustain the congregation's interest after the central point has been made, because some people's minds begin to wander once there is no longer any suspense. But skillfully handled, as it almost invariably was by Brooks, the method is without parallel in getting across and hammering home the single truth of a sermon. By the time the preacher has examined three or four facets of the truth—has held the jewel in the light and turned it for all to see—there can be no one in the audience who has missed it.

6. *The experimental sermon.* This is a general category to include the wide variety of sermon types that have appeared on the homiletical scene in the past two or three decades:

Dialogue sermons
Dramatic monologues
Epistolary sermons
Parable sermons
Sermons from novels and plays
Sermons in verse

Mime sermons
Slide shows
News report sermons
Musical sermons
Etc.

Experimentation is healthy, both for the preacher and for the congregation. On the preacher's side, freedom from more traditional forms permits us to hear and see in ways we have not heard and seen before; we actually perceive the gospel in new ways when we work with different methods. On the congregation's side, new forms of preaching develop alertness to the communication process; it becomes necessary to *notice* the sermon and how it handles the message; it is no longer possible merely to sleep through the sermon time.

Individual experimental methods have their own particular advantages. Media sermons — using drama, slides, movies — enable people to see as well as hear. Such sermons bring the gospel into the right brain as well as into the left, where images take hold of the person and aid in total conversion. News report sermons, dealing with items currently on people's minds, have contemporaneity that is hard to beat. Dialogue sermons, usually between two persons but sometimes between the preacher and an alter ego, permit the raising of contrary viewpoints in creative and helpful ways. Epistolary sermons have a kind of intimacy that is useful in dealing with certain subjects.

One of the most powerful epistolary sermons I ever heard was one preached by Jerry L. Barnes, who was, at the time of the war in Vietnam, pastor of the University Baptist Church in Shawnee, Oklahoma. There was a munitions plant near Shawnee, and many members of University Baptist Church were associated with the plant. There were also many college students in the church, and most of them were strongly antiwar. The munitions workers, who paid most of the bills in the church, could not understand the antiwar position and resented the presence of the college students in their midst. In an effort to mediate understanding and defuse a potentially dangerous confrontation, Dr. Barnes preached a

Christmas sermon called "A Christmas Eve Letter."[9] Following the tape-recorded sounds of tracer bullets, mortar fire, and sporadic bombing and accompanied by the soft playing of "I Heard the Bells on Christmas Day," Dr. Barnes read a letter from a young soldier to his parents in which he described the senselessness of the war he was seeing and talked about how much he wanted to be back home. Then a letter from the young man's mother was read, commenting on the prosperity of folks around the munitions plant, telling about the new room they had added to the house with the father's overtime money, and generally missing out on any real communication with the son. Finally, there was a brief message from the Department of Defense, announcing to the parents that their son had been killed. Following the worship service, there was a forum discussion of the issues raised in the sermon. Both the munitions people and the students understood each other better, and their relationship in the church markedly improved.

Every preacher should, on occasion, attempt an experimental sermon. If it does nothing else, it will keep an edge of creativity on the preacher's soul so that he or she does not automatically fall into a routine method of approaching every sermon theme. It will take some effort, especially if the form involves the coordination of media with the sermon or rehearsal with other persons who may be involved. But the efforts will be worth it in terms of sharpened perceptions and new discoveries.

ANOTHER LOOK AT
THE DEVELOPMENTAL METHOD

Competent architects are never limited to a single style of building. They may be working simultaneously on several buildings with varied styles — a tall, sleek skyscraper in Manhattan; a low, Japanese-styled resort in California; a boxy, cantilevered office building in St. Louis. But most architects also have a single style with which they are most thoroughly acquainted and comfortable. It is to this style that they return when all other factors are equal and they are free to work as they like. It is, in a manner of speaking, their "bread and butter" style.

The same is true of preachers. Their versatility should be apparent over the years as they turn to various methods of preaching sermons. But underlying their entire preaching ministries is a single style that is reliable and comfortable to them — one that fits their work the way an old slipper fits the foot. For most preachers that style is the developmental sermon. It is no accident that it has been a favorite preaching form for centuries. The form did not simply happen. It evolved through the ministries of many persons as a method supremely suited for doing what the preacher needs to do when he or she gets in the pulpit. It remains the single most useful style of sermon making and is likely to be so, with minor changes, a hundred years from now.

It is important, therefore, that we take a closer look at the developmental method of preaching. If it is the preacher's "bread and butter" method, it deserves careful study.

The first thing to consider is the matter of outline, of arriving at the basic substructure of the sermon. A few well-known preachers, like Eugene Carson Blake, have paid little attention to structure in their sermons. Blake said that in his preparation to preach he thought about his subject until he felt quite saturated with it, then commenced to write out the sermon. Sometimes he jotted down three or four words on a paper as major guideposts, but usually he simply plunged into writing. Most prominent preachers, however, have sworn by the significance of a good outline before beginning to write. It is in the outline, they say, that the real strength and beauty of a sermon lie. The outline of a sermon is like the frame of a house — it provides the architectural soundness without which not even the most expensive decoration would be suitable.

Halford Luccock, who often put things memorably, said: "The fear of the Lord is the beginning of wisdom in preaching, but the fear of gelatin also helps."[10]

There are several advantages to having a good outline. First, the soundness of the total sermon may be tested and the outline adjusted, if necessary, before one makes the major investment of writing time in the sermon. It is much easier to tear up an outline than to give up an entire sermon once it has been completed. Moreover, the validity of ideas and the movement of the sermon are much easier to judge in this skeletal stage than later in the full manuscript. If the climax appears to arrive too early in the sermon, a little work on the outline will rearrange matters so that it comes at the appropriate place. If a point is weak in the sequence of ideas, its weakness can be spotted and attended to in the outline. Even the placement of illustrations can be managed more adroitly at this stage. Somehow it is much harder to see all the important details in full perspective when the manuscript is finished; at this point it is like being lost in the woods, when one could have had an aerial view of things before setting out.

Second, a good outline helps the preacher get and keep a grasp of the sermon both in the composition and in the preaching of it. What a comfort it is in the middle of writing a sermon, when one has expatiated for half a page on some point and feels momentarily depleted or lost, to be able to revert to the outline and say, "Ah, there is where I must go next!" Likewise, when the sermon is being delivered, it is encouraging to be able to drop one's eye to the outline and think, "There's the next point I must make; I am glad to be on course with my thoughts."

Third and equally important, a well-constructed outline gives clues to the congregation about the progress of the sermon and also helps the congregation to fix the sermon in their memories so that it becomes "portable." This does not mean that the divisions of a sermon should always be announced to the congregation, the way a train conductor calls out stops along the way. But even when the structure is unannounced, the congregation perceives it, the way passengers on a train note their progress on the journey; they have a sense of movement, of direction, and find this inwardly assuring.

BRAINSTORMING

Let us suppose that the preacher gets an idea for a sermon, either from some germ in a notebook or from a lectionary text, has arrived at a succinct statement of purpose for the sermon, and wishes to proceed to an outline. What is the next step to take? One could, of course, proceed directly to formulating the major points of the sermon, and sometimes the mind will provide these points without much effort. But many preachers find it helpful at this juncture to pause and see how many thoughts and ideas they can summon that might have any bearing whatsoever on the general theme of the sermon. Some, like Sangster, even take this step before defining their statement of purpose. We are talking about brainstorming, of course—a technique for eliciting from the mind all the ideas and combinations of ideas it is so amply capable of storing. Many sermons are lacking in interesting material simply because preachers have not learned systematically to assemble the thoughts and illustrations that would enrich them.

The shortest distance between two points, if those points are the idea for a sermon and the completed sermon, is not necessarily a straight line. Often it is the most meandering, leisurely kind of line that can be imagined. At this point of the sermon-making process, the preacher can be immensely helped by dreaming, fantasizing, and indulging in unhurried reflection. The trick is to shut off the left side of the brain, which is the no-nonsense, rational, matter-of-fact side, and give full power to the right side, where flights of fancy originate. The preacher's writing hand should be busy, taking down notes on these unscheduled flights. There should be absolutely no censoring of what is written down. The minute one begins to say, "That is crazy; I'll not write that down," the whole creative process is inhibited; flags begin going down on ideas that might have proven valuable if given a place on the paper. The process is akin to what the surrealists in the early part of our century call "automatic" writing, in which a poet went into a trance and wrote everything that came into his or her head. In the preacher's case, the mind should be free to travel everywhere at once, ransacking past experiences, books, friendships, and everything else that might yield up some idea or anecdote potentially useful to the sermon. Scriptures with any possible bearing on the theme should be noted, even though the preacher may be working from a lectionary text. Before he or she is through—after thirty minutes or an hour of wild, unmanaged mind travel—there should be a page full of phrases and ideas. Some will appear only remotely related to the purpose of the sermon. Others will prove invaluable.

A picture is supposed to be worth ten thousand words. Let's see how such a brainstorming session might look once its effects are down on paper. Suppose the preacher has both a text and a statement of purpose. The text is Luke 22:54–62, the story of Peter's denial of his relationship to Jesus. The purpose of the sermon to be preached is *to encourage people who have failed in their Christian vows to renew their devotion to Christ*. The brainstorming will probably focus on one, two or possibly three general areas: failure, vows, and renewal. This is not to inhibit the process in any way, but to provide some starting points. Try making your own list of ideas and illustrations based on this. Then compare it with the following list:

Richard Bach tried dozens of publishers before finding one for *Jonathan Livingston Seagull*.

Time I failed to stop a wrong to another person.

Judas also failed — but couldn't accept forgiveness.

DiMaggio's string of 56 hits, then 13 misses — received a five-minute ovation in Fenway Park, then boos and catcalls in Yankee Stadium — said, "They never boo a bum."

Failure also physical — loss of stamina and power, especially as one grows older.

Failure to understand — teenage boy crying at father's funeral, "Dad, I *tried* to get you to understand."

Failure of love — not loving or caring enough.

Sense of failure and shame in a nation — Vietnam.

Shame I felt when failing a vital catch in a ball game.

Christ himself may have felt failure — at least he appeared to fail in his mission to Israel.

Two kinds of failure in parable of prodigal son — the prodigal's and the elder brother's.

Physiochemical failures — coach who studied his batters and noted they used the same swing during a slump as at other times, so linked it to chemical imbalances in body.

The joy of forgiveness and reacceptance.

Inadvertent failures — when we don't know someone else is counting on us or needing us — time I let down a friend's wife.

Story of two enemies who came to reconciliation over Communion table.

Greater shame felt when we fail in a specific vow as Peter did ("I'll never leave you").

Prodigal son's acceptance by the father.

Hosea's acceptance of Gomer after adulteries.

The great Babe Ruth struck out 1,316 times.

Living with failure and what it does to one's character.

How often Edison failed on way to success — and the Curies!

Do you see how a list like this makes the preacher's adrenaline flow? Who couldn't begin to put together a sermon from a page full of ideas and illustrations like this? The point is, any preacher with a little imagination and experience can compose such a list. There is nothing esoteric or difficult about it. All it requires is a little relaxation in which the mind is given its freedom to roam over the subject area and offer suggestions.

The preacher who has any trouble composing a brainstorming list is advised to try some method other than merely sitting at a desk and trying to accomplish the task in an hour or so. Some persons find that it helps if they sleep on a matter, then get up and go at it again the next day. This permits the unconscious mind to put some ideas on the dumbwaiter and send them up into consciousness. Others like to make their lists as they go about their weekly tasks. A pocket notebook, even the one used to jot down sermon ideas, can provide a handy place for recording things that come to mind.

Many ministers have learned in recent years the value of having a congregational group to help in this brainstorming project. It is amazing to see how much richer group experience is than individual experience on almost any subject one can imagine. And it goes without saying that the richer one's list of materials, the richer the sermon itself is likely to be.

PRODUCING AN OUTLINE

Once the preacher has a good brainstorm list in hand, there are two methods of getting from it to the sermon outline — one indirect and the other direct.

The *indirect* method involves brooding over the list of materials until an outline begins to take shape in the mind. In this method the list serves as a springboard to the outline, and there is no attempt to get as much material as possible from the list into the final outline. The list is a resource, but does not necessarily determine the shape of the outline or the bulk of the content. For example, the preacher may be struck by the contrast between what happened to Judas and what happened to Peter after they failed, and build the entire sermon around that idea.

The *direct* method is to look for "clustering" in the material, that is, to find relationships among the various items on the list and to group the items according to these relationships. For example, in the list above (pages 63–64), the following natural groupings might be seen to occur:

Richard Bach, etc.
Joe DiMaggio's "They never boo a bum"
Christ himself may have felt a failure, etc.
Physiochemical failures — slumps and successes, etc.
Inadvertent failures (maybe also inadvertent successes)
Babe Ruth's strikeouts
Edison's and the Curies' failures

Time I failed to stop a wrong
Failure also physical — loss of stamina, etc.
Failure to understand, etc.
Failure of love, etc.
Sense of shame in a nation — Vietnam
Christ himself may have felt failure

Two kinds of failure in prodigal son
Physiochemical failures, etc.
Inadvertent failures
Babe Ruth's strikeouts
Edison's and the Curies' failures

Judas also failed—but couldn't accept forgiveness
Living with failure—what it does to one's character

The joy of forgiveness and reacceptance
The two enemies who came to reconciliation over Communion table
The prodigal son's acceptance by the father
Hosea's acceptance of Gomer after adulteries

Some items are included in more than one group. As in the case of "inadvertent failures," an item will also occasionally grow or evolve while being considered for inclusion in one group or another. Remain flexible at this point. Let your imagination continue to introduce material and see new meanings and relationships.

The next step in the direct method is to give some kind of name to each of the groupings—a form of identification that more or less embraces all the items in a group. In the groupings above, everything in the first group has to do with failures that either were or became successes; suppose we call this group "Failure as Prelude to Success." The second grouping is about many kinds of failures, both personal and societal, physical and spiritual, intentional and unintentional; let's call it "Failure as a Common Experience." The third grouping, a small one, is about "The Tragedy of Failure." And the final group is about acceptance after failure; we could simply call it "Acceptance After Failure," or, because of the religious associations of the items in the group, "The Religious Uses of Failure."

Now look at the titles we have given the groups. Do they suggest anything about the form of the sermon? Could they be arranged in such a way as actually to constitute the sermon? Play with them a bit. "Failure as Prelude to Success" is not a good way to start a sermon using the other groups, for it is one of the more positive notes, and the other groupings would seem to go downhill from it. Which group would serve as a good starting place? "The Tragedy of Failure" might, but it is a rather minor grouping. "Failure as a Common Experience" would also work, and it is a major grouping. Perhaps reflection leads us to see the value of beginning with this group of ideas; we could easily involve our hearers in the subject here, for failure has been an experience of theirs. So we have a point of beginning. Where do we go next? The logic of movement suggests that "The Tragedy of Failure" would follow the first grouping. That leaves two groups, "Failure as Prelude to Success" and "The Religious Uses of Failure." Which of these should come next and which last? We reexamine the entries under each heading. It's a toss-up; we could imagine concluding the sermon with either group.

At this point of the process it may be a good idea to lay the material aside for a few hours and forget about it, then return to it with a fresh mind. That is often a good technique when one is not getting anywhere with a sermon. Or you can play with the groupings some more and possibly come up with alternate arrangements. Maybe what these group titles need is more structural uniformity. What if we set up the sermon like this:

    I. Failure as a Common Experience
   II. Failure as a Tragic Experience
  III. Failure as a Prelude to Success
  IV. Failure as the Place Where We Meet Christ
       (formerly "The Religious Uses of Failure")

We might be satisfied with this arrangement, or we might continue to work at it. Perhaps we could simplify it a bit. We don't have much material under "Failure as a Tragic Experience"; suppose we omitted that section. It *is* rather obvious, isn't it? Everyone knows how tragic failure can be; we don't need to underscore that for them. All right, let's drop II. That will tighten the outline and leave us with this arrangement:

I. Failure as a Common Experience

II. Failure as a Prelude to Success

III. Failure as the Place Where We Meet Christ

Is that the best we can do? Perhaps we feel that there is something still not quite right about it. We reflect some more. What if we reversed the order of II and III? Let's try that and see what the results appear to be:

I. Failure as a Common Experience

II. Failure as the Place Where We Meet Christ

III. Failure as a Prelude to Success

Ah, that seems a little stronger. The mood seems to swing upward more consistently this way: from our failures to meeting Christ to becoming successes. Let's try it that way.

There is one more step to go. We must get an introduction, decide on the specific material to be used under each point we have chosen, and draw everything to an appropriate conclusion. What would constitute a good introduction? Which items under the three headings should go and which remain? How could the remaining items be arranged for best effect? And which item, if any, would make a compelling conclusion?

Let's think first about the introduction. It should quickly and easily draw the congregation into sympathy with the entire theme of the sermon. Maybe an illustration of failure would do this. What are the possibilities? "Sense of failure in a nation" is too broad. It is also controversial, as the entire Vietnam War was controversial. Best not to begin with that. How about "Time I failed to stop a wrong" or "Failure to understand — teenage boy crying at father's funeral, etc."? Either would probably get people's attention, but we sense one problem with them — they are *heavy*. They have a depressing effect and are not very inviting for an opener. Then how about something lighter, the one about "Shame I felt in failing a catch in a ball game"? That has a humorous side to it. Besides, it's personal. The preacher can begin the sermon with a "confession," and that permits other people to think about their failures without feeling that they are under attack. They can identify with the speaker. Good, let's go with that. We can begin there and easily move into the first point of the sermon, about the commonness of failure.

You have seen enough of the process now for me to move quickly to a possible outline for the sermon using the materials we have discussed. Other outlines are of course possible—one of the intriguing aspects of sermon building is making the hundreds of small decisions that have to be made—but this is one way the final outline might appear:

"Failure Can Be a Good Experience"
Introduction: Shame I felt when I missed a catch in a ball game.

I. Failure as a Common Experience
We all fail sometimes
Even Babe Ruth struck out many times
Physiochemical failures and aging account for unavoidable failure
Peter remains a symbol of our spiritual failure

II. Failure as the Place Where We Meet Christ
Peter's failure brought confrontation with self and Jesus
Jesus understood failure—even appeared to fail himself
Jesus set forgiveness and reacceptance of the failed person at center of the gospel (cf. story of prodigal son)
He forgave and recommissioned Peter
He will do same for us

III. Failure as a Prelude to Success
Failure not bad if understood from this perspective
Means a greater understanding of what it is to be human
DiMaggio took it in stride: "They never boo a bum"
Edison's many failures on way to success
Contrast between Judas and Peter: Judas couldn't accept forgiveness; Peter did, and became a leader in early church

Conclusion: Illustration of enemies who were reconciled over Communion table; this is where we realize we have been enemies of Christ and are reconciled, then go out to serve

It is debatable whether this is the best conclusion. I have chosen it on the assumption that the sermon is to be followed by Holy Communion. If it is not, then a simple conclusion arising from the final remarks of the third point would probably be preferable. The preacher might say, for example: "We have been talking about failure. I am afraid that I have failed in this sermon. I find it very hard to succeed as I would like to in talking about our problems as human beings and the way God accepts and loves us despite our failures. But God does. Just as Jesus accepted Peter's failure and gave him mighty things to do for God, you are accepted in your failure and given important things to do. The worst failure of all is not anything we have done or failed to do in the past. It is the failure to accept new life when it is offered to us — as it is offered now."

WHAT TO LOOK FOR IN
THE OUTLINE

Now the outline is complete. Suppose you have had a great idea for a sermon. You have studied your text carefully and listened to it sensitively. You have considered your congregation and decided upon the emphasis that will bring text and human need together. You have thought keenly about this emphasis until you have been able to capture the purpose of the entire sermon in a single, glistening sentence. Then you have brainstormed the theme until you produced a page full of ideas, references, and anecdotes or illustrations applicable to it. Finally, you brooded over these resources until an outline emerged from them, and you have before you the skeleton of a sermon — ideas properly clustered and illustrations clearly indicated. You are ready to take a critical look at the outline to see whether your architecture is sound before you proceed to the final building of the sermon. What do you look for?

First, you look for the theological validity of the whole sermon. How well does the sermon represent the text? Does it gather up the

entire sense of the passage, so that the theological thrust of the biblical author is embodied in the sermon, or does it express a mere
fragment of the text? To be sure, there may be times when you
intend to express only a part of the text; but a careful examination
of the outline will verify whether you have failed to represent the
text fairly when you actually thought you were doing so. The most
powerful preaching has a strong biblical orientation, whether the
text is either partially or fully employed; and the outline is the
stage of the sermon preparation where this is most readily assessed.

Second, you look for the personal helpfulness of the sermon.
Have you really achieved what you set out to do in your statement
of purpose, to provide a solution to some important problem trou-
bling the minds and hearts of your hearers? A preacher often discovers at this stage that he or she has gotten caught up in the
academic theology of the text or in the rhetoric of the outline and
has failed to set forth the gospel in a practical or useful way. If that
is the case, the outline needs to go back to the drawing board.
Points and illustrations require realignment so that the finished
sermon will wing its way into eager hearts.

Third, the outline is the place to look first for the clarity of the
sermon. If it is not simple and clear, there is little hope that the
sermon written from it will be simple and clear. One can hardly
drape contemporary Western architecture, with its clean, func-
tional lines, on a substructure of Gothic scaffolding. Be sure that
every word in the main points of the outline is strong and direct,
that every phrase is orderly, that every sentence is simple and
lucid, as pure as you can make them. Then the development of the
sermon will be strong and precise, and people will have a sense of
its progression from idea to idea.

Fourth, examine the outline for its balance and proportion. Is
there an appropriate symmetry in the parts of the sermon, or does
one point seem to dominate the others in the amount of time it will
require? Is the length of the introduction suitable to the remainder
of the sermon? Now is the moment to decide whether you have
planned these matters well. It is much easier to rearrange your
outline than to try to prune an overlong section of the sermon after
it is written. You can actually determine the approximate length
of the sermon as you review your structure. Suppose you wish to

preach eighteen minutes. If there are three parts to the sermon, you may wish to think of giving five minutes to each part, plus two minutes for an introduction and a minute or two for the conclusion. If you are typing single-spaced pages, you will wish to assign about one-third of a page for the introduction, about two-thirds of a page each for the three points, and another one-fourth to one-third of a page for the conclusion. Visualizing the completed manuscript this way permits you to think out your material with an eye on its length. A competent preacher knows the importance of this kind of prearrangement. As George Sweazey has said, "Unless there is careful proportioning, a sermon on Rom. 5:20 KJV, 'Where sin abounded, grace did much more abound,' is likely to have sin abounding through three-fourths of the sermon and grace much less abounding because the time ran out."[11]

Fifth, consider whether there is good psychological progression in the outline. George Buttrick used to ask us of a sermon in class, "Does it *march?*" Will it sweep people along with a sense of its movement? Sermons that always seem to be going somewhere are much more appealing than those that merely eddy about. There is a certain amount of nervousness in congregations that is vented or dispelled by a sermon that is going someplace. But it is imploded by a sermon that isn't, and builds to more and more intolerable levels. Then the congregation becomes edgy and impatient; people begin to look at their watches, stifle yawns, and fidget in their seats. As Leslie Tizard, minister of Carrs Lane Church in Birmingham, England, said: "Once a well-constructed sermon has begun, it ought to unroll itself like a ball of wool which has no knots or tangles in it. One idea should call the next to mind by a close and natural sequence."[12]

A close and natural sequence is what we are after. Reflect on the development of the sermon to see that it is truly sequential — that one point follows another in ascending fashion. For example, suppose you are preparing a classification sermon on carrying the gospel, and you have these points: Carrying the gospel —

1. Into one's home
2. Into one's neighborhood
3. Into one's world

If you examine the outline for progression, you see that you have succeeded in arranging the points in a naturally expanding order; each proceeds to a greater point, in the manner of concentric circles spreading outward from the center.

It is possible to reverse the order of this outline thus —

1. Into one's world
2. Into one's neighborhood
3. Into one's home

— and still have a sense of progression, especially if you plan to regard the third point as the climax and enforce the idea in the congregation that the greatest test of all in carrying the gospel is what one does among those nearest to one's own heart. Sometimes it is more difficult to exemplify the gospel among those who know us than it is among those to whom we are strangers.

But it would be hard to imagine a circumstance under which anyone could wish to preach a sermon with the second point as the climactic one:

1. Into one's home
2. Into one's world
3. Into one's neighborhood

There is something psychologically wrong with this order. Instead of progressing naturally, it flips back and forth. Unless warned to the contrary, the congregation would have every right to expect that the second point is the final one, because the progression from home to the world leaves no room for further expansion.

This outline is greatly oversimplified for purposes of illustration. Seldom will the order of progression be so readily apparent to the preacher's mind. Sometimes the material that one has to marshal under the points will determine the sequence. For example, a preacher who is preparing a sermon on John 15:13, "Greater love has no man than this, that a man lay down his life for his friends," may wish to offer these three observations about love:

1. Love is blind
2. Love knows no bounds
3. Love conquers all

Reflection assures the preacher that point 1 is probably in its proper location. On an emotional scale from zero to ten, it would not rate as highly as either 2 or 3. It is more difficult, though, to decide whether 2 and 3 are properly sequenced. The distinguishing factor may lie in the material assembled under the two points. If the material under 2 is more significant emotionally than the material under 3, then the present order should definitely be reversed.

When the choices have been made well, there will be a sense of *inevitability* in the progression of the sermon. This is an important factor in any art form. A mystery story unfolds with unavoidable logic. A poem develops with just the right words. A strong piece of sculpture has lines of force that could not be controverted without impeding or even destroying its beauty. And a good sermon marches inexorably toward its conclusion, molding sense and sound together until it has accomplished its mission. People who hear it should be able to say, "I couldn't argue with that — it moved from A to B to C so naturally that it carried me along without any protest!"

For example, George Buttrick once preached a sermon on Ps. 42:1–2:

> As a hart longs for flowing streams,
>   so longs my soul for thee, O God.
> My soul thirsts for God, for the living God.
> When shall I come and behold the face of God?

Called "The Thirst for God," the sermon began with allusion to a novel called *The Great Desire.* The novel told of a young writer coming from New England to ask people in New York City, "What do you want?" Perhaps, said Buttrick, Rudyard Kipling could have given him the answer, for when he stirred restlessly in a serious sickness and the nurse asked him, "Do you want anything?" he murmured, "I want God." From there it was a simple journey through the points of the sermon:

1. The thirst for God — why should anyone have such an absurd thirst?
2. The thirst is for the "living" God
3. Why should the psalmist carry the prayer further, and long for "the face of God"?

The face of God, of course, was in Christ, and that is the substance of Buttrick's third point. "So the longing for God finds answer," he concluded, "and the thirst for God is slaked, and the yearning to see the face of God is satisfied—as much as mortal man may ask, God mercifully veiled in our flesh, until hereafter we see Him face to face."[13]

The sermon has a marvelous economy. Each point leads naturally to the next, and the whole is integrally related to the text. The effect is nicely cumulative: the sermon gathers strength and momentum as it goes.

Paul Scherer, Buttrick's contemporary, preached an intriguing sermon called "Scandals of Faith."[14] Its text was Matt. 8:1-10, in which Jesus healed a leper and a centurion's servant. "Lord, if thou wilt, thou canst make me clean," said the leper. Scherer played with this a bit. There was no doubt in the leper's mind that Christ could heal him. But would he? That was the question. This is also, suggested Scherer, our question.

What if (and this became point 1 of the sermon) *God is power without love*—without the will to heal us? This point was explored. *What if, on the other hand* (point 2), *God is love without power?* This would be as bad as the other, to have a God with the intention of healing but without the resources to do it. Ah, but *what if* (the final point) *God were power in love with us*—power made personal and shown as compassionate in Jesus Christ?

It is a superb outline, developed on a Hegelian framework of thesis, antithesis, and synthesis. It is clear and memorable, so that people can reconstruct it in their minds and ponder it long after it has been preached. It also has a marvelous sense of inevitability about it, as if every point were just as it ought to be and could not be altered without destroying the force and symmetry of the entire sermon.

SERMONS LIKE DRAMAS

The movement of the form of a good sermon is similar to that of a Shakespearean play. A Shakespearean tragedy always begins with something interesting; those were rough days in the theater, and the playwright had to get the audience's attention. Then it begins to build as the plot thickens. The graph line develops slowly, rising steadily. Then, because audiences do not like uninterrupted learning times and become impatient at receiving mere information, there is momentary relief, usually through some comic scene that breaks the tension.

In the sermon, the tension breaker may be a bit of humor or, more likely, an illustration. People relax during an illustration; they can follow it more easily than they can follow other parts of the sermon. One can almost see the relaxation of tension in their faces.

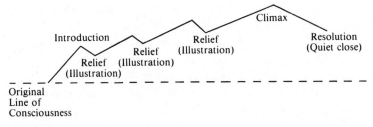

Then the plot thickens some more; information is increased. The graph line goes up. The preacher and the playwright are both getting serious.

But wait! Someone on fourth row center has dropped out; she has absorbed all she can for the time being. More relief! So Shakespeare has another comic scene; the preacher uses another illustration. That did it, she's showing interest again.

Onward with the serious material. More building, more relief.

Finally, a climax. In Shakespeare's *Othello*, for example, Othello murders Desdemona; the audience is electrified. In the sermon, the preacher clinches an emotional argument for the commitment of the hearers; they are sitting on the edges of their seats, breathless and ecstatic.

Notice in both cases how far above the original line of consciousness we have risen. The building has been slow, perhaps at times almost imperceptible. But we are now in a different atmosphere than when we began.

After the climax, a slight winding down occurs. Shakespeare

never ended a play at full zenith. He was too good a psychologist for that. He knew that people could not bear to be sent away immediately after a murder; there must be time for resolution, for appropriating the wisdom of the play, for internalizing the action. The same is true of the sermon. "Cultivate the quiet close," says James Stewart of Scotland. "Let your last words of appeal have in them something of the hush that falls when Christ Himself draws near."[15] This way people turn to the remainder of the liturgy calmly and with true resolution.

Does this seem too artificial, too calculated, to be used by the Spirit of God? Consider how often the Spirit has used great preachers in precisely this manner.

"Art is limitation," said Chesterton; "the essence of every picture is the frame. If you draw a giraffe, you must draw him with a long neck. If, in your bold creative way, you hold yourself free to draw a giraffe with a short neck, you will really find that you are not free to draw a giraffe. The moment you step into the world of facts, you step into a world of limits."[16] The same is true of preaching a sermon. We are free to do it any way we please—until we step into the world of facts and learn what works and what doesn't. Then we will come back to the basic laws of sermon outlining. Our real freedom lies in the projection of our personalities through the material we use and the way we speak, not in our ability to flout the rules of effective preaching.

NOTES

1. James Pike, *A New Look in Preaching* (New York: Charles Scribner's Sons, 1961), p. 71.

2. Robert J. Smithson, ed., *My Way of Preaching* (London: Pickering and Inglis, n.d.), p. 131.

3. John Henry Jowett, *The Preacher, His Life and Work* (New York: George H. Doran, 1912), p. 133.

4. Smithson, ed., *My Way of Preaching*, pp. 131–32.

5. John R. Fry, *Fire and Blackstone* (Philadelphia: J. B. Lippincott Co., 1969).

6. Ibid., p. 22.

7. Clovis Chappell, *The Village Tragedy and Other Sermons* (Nashville: Abingdon-Cokesbury Press, 1925), p. 82.

8. Phillips Brooks, *Twenty Sermons* (New York: E. P. Dutton & Co., 1903), pp. 60–75.

9. In John Killinger, ed., *Experimental Preaching* (Nashville: Abingdon Press, 1973), pp. 111–15. For other experimental sermons, see John Killinger, ed., *The 11 O'Clock News and Other Experimental Sermons* (Nashville: Abingdon Press, 1975).

10. Halford Luccock, *In the Minister's Workshop* (Nashville: Abingdon-Cokesbury Press, 1944), p. 121.

11. George Sweazey, *Preaching the Good News* (Englewood Cliffs, N.J.: Prentice-Hall, 1976), p. 117.

12. Smithson, ed., *My Way of Preaching*, p. 167.

13. George A. Buttrick, *Sermons Preached in a University Church* (Nashville: Abingdon Press, 1959), pp. 157–163.

14. In Paul Scherer, *The Word God Sent* (New York: Harper & Row, 1965), pp. 169–177.

15. James S. Stewart, *Heralds of God: A Practical Book on Preaching* (New York: Charles Scribner's Sons, 1956), pp. 139–140.

16. G. K. Chesterton, *Orthodoxy* (New York: Doubleday & Co., Image Books, 1959), p. 40.

Beginnings and Endings

"It is an idle question," says W. E. Sangster, "whether the beginning or the end of a sermon is more important. If you do not get the people's attention, nothing you say will make any difference. If you get their attention and do not put it to the highest use, you will have failed to make the occasion 'a maximum for God.' "[1]

We have all heard sermons in which the preacher seemed unable to get into the matter to be dealt with and sermons in which he or she seemed unable to get out. Nothing makes a congregation more uncomfortable. Most skilled preachers, therefore, pay particular attention to the crafting of beginnings and endings for their sermons. They know that an apt beginning is like a good approach shot to the green: it puts them a comfortable distance from the pin. They also know that a good ending is like an accurate putt: it wraps up the game in the fewest possible strokes. Consequently they work hard to make these parts of the sermon as deft and effective as possible.

MAKING A START

A good beginning at anything—a race, a novel, a concerto—is important. To start badly is to start with a handicap. Often it can mean the difference between being successful and being unsuccessful at an undertaking. "If only I could start over," people are heard to complain when they have failed, " I think I could do much better." The secret is to start well the first time.

The beginning of the sermon is no exception. It does much to set the tone and mood for the sermon. If it accomplishes its purposes, people are well on their way to hearing the sermon; if it doesn't, the rest of the sermon will be uphill.

J. Randall Nichols in *Building the Word* speaks of the introduction as the "contract" between the preacher and the congregation. It is the time when the preacher suggests to the congregation what he or she wishes to treat in the sermon and gains the congregation's willing participation in what is to follow. If the contract is not established, communication of the sermon will be very difficult.[2]

Even the preacher's mood is affected by the introduction. If the opening remarks are effective, the preacher feels confident and relaxed; he or she shifts into second gear and moves easily into the body of the sermon. A poor beginning, on the other hand, absorbs psychic energy the preacher needs for continuing the sermon. He or she has a feeling of awkwardness, of not making it, of not being on the right wavelength with the congregation. Like a runner tripped at the start of a race, the preacher has a hard time regaining balance.

Sometimes an introduction comes easily. It may even have occurred in the preacher's mind at the time when the idea for the sermon came. At other times it comes only with difficulty, long after the body of the sermon has taken shape. Some ministers purposely delay writing the introduction until last so that they know precisely what it is they are going to introduce. Others make a practice of returning to the introduction, once they have completed the sermon, to be sure that it still functions effectively in relation to the whole. Either way, they underscore the importance of making a good beginning.

Robert McCracken, who was preaching minister at Riverside Church, said that even after a quarter century in the ministry he still had to work assiduously at the introductions of his sermons, often spending an entire morning to produce one. He wished every word to be right, so that each sentence was a sharpened tool for digging immediately into his subject. With the vast and critical audience he was accustomed to facing, he knew that anything less might lose the battle before it was begun.[3]

80

CHARACTERISTICS OF A
GOOD BEGINNING

Introductions can be as varied as the sermons they introduce and the preachers who devise them. Carlyle Marney, six months after being struck by a heart attack and carried from the pulpit of Myers Park Baptist Church in Charlotte, North Carolina, began his next sermon, "As I was saying . . ." Sangster tells about J. N. Figgis's sermon at the University of Cambridge in June 1918, when the Allies were being driven back in Europe. In an atmosphere of national fear, he read his text, "The Lord sitteth upon the flood; yea, the Lord sitteth King for ever" (Ps. 29:10 KJV), and began his sermon with one tense question: "Does he? Does he?"[4] John Fry, on the other hand, preached a sermon at First Presbyterian Church of Chicago in which the introduction ran two and one-half of the sermon's eight and one-half pages. The sermon was called "Supertrumping," and Fry began by explaining the principle of supertrumps in bridge, then telling of an incident in which a group of campus pastors hoodwinked an Old Testament specialist into believing in the existence of a "world-famous" authority on the Book of Amos whom they had invented. The sermon was based on Deut. 19:16-21 and Mark 13:9-27, both of which passages predicted dire consequences for the enemies of God, which Fry said were "objectively untrue" but very useful to the purposes of those who invented them.[5]

It is possible, however, to adduce certain general characteristics of effective introductions and to bear these in mind when we are designing the beginnings of our sermons. The good preacher is conscious of these hallmarks even when he or she chooses to ignore them, and, more often than not, bows to them in the preparation of introductions.

First, the best introductions are usually brief. They do not usurp time needed for the substance of the sermon itself. Like a good master of ceremonies, they set up the audience for the next guest, then quickly bow out of the way. George Buttrick disciplined us in his sermon classes by requiring that we write our introductions

81

in fifty words or less. His own introductions are seldom that brief, but neither are they very lengthy. Normally they run between one hundred and one hundred and fifty words.

Consider this one for a sermon called "Lonely Voyage":

> Rupert Brooke, taking ship from Liverpool to New York, felt suddenly lonely, for he seemed the only passenger without friends on the dock to wave him good-bye. So he ran back down the gangplank, picked out an urchin, and asked, "What's your name?" "Bill," said the boy. "Well, Bill, you are my friend, and here is sixpence. Wave to me when the ship goes." The boy waved a handkerchief in a very grubby hand. Our human voyage is a still lonelier affair. The ship of this strange planet—should we say of the cosmos?—plunges on its way with no apparent port of departure, for nobody knows how or where or why our human life began; and no apparent port of arrival, for every passenger is buried in the deep. We are on a lonely voyage. When we confront that fact, biblical faith begins.[6]

One hundred forty-four words, and the sermon is well launched!

Second, good introductions are usually arresting. They compel attention with interesting information or piquant statements. In the language of the songwriter, they *hook* the audience. They say, in effect, "Here is something you want to listen to, something you will be glad you heard." Edmund Steimle preached a sermon for the Sunday after Christmas, for example, called "From Bethlehem to Bedlam," that began this way:

> Back in England at the opening of the fifteenth century, a priory for the order of the Star of Bethlehem began to take in some patients and in time became the Bethlehem Hospital in London—the first lunatic asylum, as they called it then, in England. Over the years, Bethlehem became shortened and slurred into Bedlam and Bedlam thus became the name for any lunatic asylum and thence a name for wild uproar and confusion. From Bethlehem to Bedlam.
>
> And that's what we've done on this day after Christmas, turned from Bethlehem—like a priory, a refuge for monks and nuns, quiet, reflective, serene—to Bedlam, a place for lunatics, a madhouse.[7]

The idea is luminous. It sheds light on the mood we are usually in after Christmas. It invites us to listen further.

Third, good introductions are often memorable. Like Steimle's, they leave us with an image or an idea that will later help us to recall the entire sermon. When asked to recall the one sermon in their lifetimes that impressed them most, many persons remember a sermon that began with a controlling metaphor or image whose stamp was on the entire sermon. For example, I always associate Leslie Weatherhead's preaching ministry with one sermon. It was called "Key Next Door." The texts were John 13:7, "Jesus said, 'Thou shalt understand hereafter,'" and 1 Cor. 13:12, "Now I know in part, but then I shall know fully." Weatherhead began by telling about a time when he wished to get inside a certain house to see what it was like. He walked around it and formed some assumptions about it, but there were many things he could not know without actually getting inside. Then he discovered a card in a window that said, "Key Next Door." He went further down the block, obtained the key, came back and entered the house. "It seems to me," said Weatherhead,

> that this is a parable. The house of life's meaning is like that. So many doors are shut, so many windows fastened. We peep in and we get glimpses of meaning. By walking round we may get a general idea of the lie of the house but there are bound to be many things that puzzle us and upon which no clear light shines. Yet, if I may press the parable, there is a notice that says, "Key Next Door." We may have to go farther on, perhaps even into the next phase of being, and indeed, perhaps the next phase after that—for there must be many stages of spiritual progress—before we can understand all, but we are promised that at last we shall understand. "Thou shalt understand hereafter."[8]

The metaphor is entwined with the sermon all the way through. In fact, the last words of the sermon, except for four brief lines of poetry, are, "The key is next door." It is impossible to forget such a sermon.

Finally—and we see this in Weatherhead's sermon too—*a good introduction is conductive.* It leads people into the sermon. It does not pose an image or an idea for its own sake, then leave it dangling at the start of the sermon. Inexperienced preachers sometimes do this. They get a brilliant notion for an introduction—something that really elicits attention—then turn almost at a ninety-degree angle to get into the fuller content of the sermon, leaving the congregation to wonder what the connection was. This kind of practice is bound to be disastrous in the long run. It is like the story of the boy who cried "Wolf! Wolf!" when there was no wolf. The preacher says, "Listen! Listen! You are going to hear a great sermon." But after a few deceptive beginnings, when there was nothing of substance to follow, the crowd learns not to pay any attention. Then, if the preacher does occasionally have a real sermon to follow the arresting introduction, the people are not listening. They learned long ago not to be taken in by promising beginnings.

One test for conductivity in the introduction is the ease with which you can refer to the introduction during the body and conclusion of the sermon. If it seems natural to repeat some phrase or question from the introduction, as Weatherhead does in "Key Next Door," you know there is an integral relation between the beginning and the rest of the sermon. If it does not—especially in the conclusion—then it is advisable to reconsider whether the introduction does in fact introduce the sermon.

EXAMPLES OF INTRODUCTIONS

There are no unbreakable rules about composing introductions. We have already noted that there are a great variety of ways to begin a sermon. Often the genius of a particular introduction will result from the creative inspiration of the preacher, and there is no accounting for inspiration. It is possible, though, in reviewing sermons by contemporary ministers, to note some of the more popular kinds of introductions. There are doubtless many other kinds. But even the brief list to follow may be helpful to the minister who is having difficulty conceiving the introduction to a sermon; he or she can run mentally through this checklist, asking, "Suppose I tried this method of getting started—would that do the trick for this particular sermon?"

1. *The focusing introduction.* This is one of the most commonly used methods of introducing a sermon. It consists of apt reflections

on the textual lesson that will help the congregation to focus on a particular aspect of the text that the preacher wishes to deal with in the sermon. It functions like a zoom lens on a camera, carrying the viewer (in this case the hearer) in for a close-up view of something the preacher plans to examine. Here, for example, is the beginning of a sermon by Herbert Farmer called "Life's Frustrations." Farmer's text was Deut. 34:1–8, which is the story of Moses' being shown the Promised Land he was not allowed to enter. Said Farmer:

> This picture of Moses, at the point of death, gazing at the Promised Land, to which through the long, arduous years he had led his beloved people, but into which he himself was never to enter, has always laid hold of the imagination of mankind. The simplicity and reticence of the Scripture words assist the powerful impression which is made. There is no attempt to match tragic words to a tragic happening, still less to draw an edifying moral. We are simply led into the presence of the old man as he sits on the mountain-top, conscious that the end is very near, and that the fruit of all his anguish and labour is to be plucked and enjoyed by another, and there we are left. We will not attempt to probe his thoughts, for he has been a giant among men, with the cords of destiny running through his fingers, and we are so small. We can only feel, somewhat inarticulately perhaps, that here is summed up all the tragic element, all the element of frustration and disappointment in life, which neither the great nor small amongst us ever escapes. There is, indeed, something of great art in the stark simplicity of God's irrevocable word to him: "I have caused thee to see it with thine eyes, but thou shalt not go over thither." For, as in all great art, a universal truth of life is here seized upon, and expressed in a single sublime instance of it.[9]

There is something almost surgical in the precision with which Farmer has sketched his beginning. The same spareness that is in the Scripture is in the introduction. We are prepared, with this simple yet majestic paragraph, to consider the whole theme of "Life's Frustrations."

2. *The informative introduction.* This too is a common form of beginning, in which the preacher provides whatever background of information is necessary to enable the hearers to understand the text and/or the sermon to follow. It may consist primarily of infor-

mation not ordinarily in the congregation's possession or, as is often the case today, of interpretive material pertaining to the text. Here is an example from a sermon by David H. C. Read entitled "The Making of a Christian." Read's text is Acts 26:28 NEB: "Agrippa said to Paul, 'You think it will not take much to win me over and make a Christian of me.'" Here is the informative manner in which he begins the sermon:

> Let me introduce the speaker: King Herod Agrippa II, last in line of a series of artful and unscrupulous politicians who made their fortunes as dishonest brokers between the Jews and the early Roman emperors. This man, Agrippa, was a kind of quisling prince who had recently added to his dominions a portion of Galilee by ingratiating himself with the Emperor Nero. Bernice, the queen at his side, was his sister with whom he had incestuous relations. She was later the mistress of Titus, the general who destroyed Jerusalem. The family life of the Herods, of whom five are mentioned in the New Testament, would provide a lifetime of material for a modern scandal sheet, and this Agrippa was perhaps the toughest specimen since Herod the Great.
>
> This, then, was the man who looked St. Paul in the face and said with a smooth irony: "You think it will not take much to win *me* over and make a Christian of me."[10]

There is vividness and helpfulness in this introduction. It provides a background against which the words of Scripture become far more dramatic than they appear at first reading.

3. *The insightful introduction.* This form of beginning features a human insight that has significance for the development of the sermon. It may come in any of several ways: a reference to a book, a quotation, a comment that was overheard, a graffito scrawled on a wall or a sidewalk, a cartoon, an inscription from a tombstone, something that happened on the way to the pulpit. Imagine, for example, this word seen on the wall of a New York subway: "God is alive and well and living at 109 Barker Street." Wouldn't that give poignancy to a text about God's involvement in our personal affairs?

The introduction with an insight in it was a favorite with J. Wallace Hamilton. Here is the beginning of his sermon called

"Drum-Major Instincts," which was based on Mark 10:37, "They said unto him, Grant unto us that we may sit, one on thy right hand, and the other on thy left hand, in thy glory":

> We all have the drum-major instinct. We all want to be important, to surpass others, to achieve distinction, to lead the parade. Or — as Carl Sandburg once put it —"We all want to play Hamlet." Alfred Adler, one of the fathers of modern psychiatry, names it the *dominant* impulse in human nature; he thinks the desire for recognition, the wish to be significant, is stronger that that of sex, which Freud put first. And while we may be provoked with James and John for asking Jesus to put them first — like soldiers holding up the battle until they have made sure of their promotion — we should in fairness admit that in a thousand subtle ways we too have tried to be drum-major.[11]

There are perhaps too many allusions in the paragraph — it fairly bristles with names. But every sentence clusters around the significant insight being propounded, and it would be hard to imagine a better launching pad for a sermon.

4. *The shocking introduction.* Sometimes a preacher will wish to command attention for a sermon by introducing it with remarks designed to provoke a shocked reaction. For example, Perry H. Biddle, Jr., once began a sermon on the mission of the church by declaring:

> The church ought to go to hell. That's right, you heard me — to hell. The church ought to go to the hell of the inner city, where crime makes decent life impossible. The church ought to go to the hell of strife-torn areas of our world, where orphans cry out at night in memory of their parents. The church ought to go to the hell of destitute places, where people are subsisting on a handful of rice a day.

Citing statistics is another way of producing a sense of shock. The preacher may give the latest figures on the U.S. defense budget — x billion dollars — and contrast them with the figures being spent on medical research, education, food for the poor, and missionary work, then preach a sermon on the priority of the kingdom of God in the lives of believers. There are obvious dangers in this method. It may verge on cuteness, insincerity, or sensationalism. But used moderately and with good intent it can be extremely effective, especially with congregations that are "hard of hearing."

5. *The confessional or personal introduction.* It was once considered bad form for a preacher to reveal his or her own personal information in a sermon. In more recent years, however, we have come to realize the importance of intimacy in communication. People want to know more about the faith and doubts of their leaders and about how their leaders cope with the ordinariness of living. Robert Raines, who was senior minister at First Community Church in Columbus, Ohio, often began sermons on an intimate note. One sermon, "Strength in Our Weakness," which later found its way into his book *To Kiss the Joy*,[12] was about God and our personal ambitions. Raines opened the sermon by telling about his great disappointment a few years earlier when he was considered and rejected for a very prestigious job. Surely everyone in the congregation knew that he had been a leading candidate for the position of preaching minister at Riverside Church in New York. His willingness to begin the sermon at the point of his own deep hurt and frustration gave a strong poignancy to the gospel's word that we are not to be anxious about the way God uses us, but to take delight in daily submission to the divine will.

Frequently a sermon can be introduced by an allusion to some less significant personal note — to the preacher's fear of flying, the preacher's difficulty with mechanical things, the preacher's war with bureaucratic red tape, or some minor quirk in the preacher's personality. I have in my notebook the outline of a sermon I plan to write one day on the phrase in the Lord's Prayer, "Give us this day our daily bread." The idea for the sermon came with the introduction in full blossom, to wit:

> I am by nature a hoarder. I discovered this recently on a trip when I took a close look at the contents of my suitcase. There were three packages of crackers I had pocketed at a restaurant. There was a package of peanuts from an airplane, plus two brightly colored napkins bearing the airline's imprint. There was a book of matches from some motel. There were two packages of jelly from the donut shop where I had eaten breakfast, and a ballpoint pen with an insurance

agent's name on it. What I realized as I gazed on this treasure trove—legal as it all was—is that I am basically nontrusting. I do not wait for "daily bread." If I had been in the wilderness with the Israelites, I would probably have been struck dead for storing manna.

The effectiveness in this introduction has to do with several things. It is low gear. It helps people to relax in the presence of the preacher because the preacher is revealing things about himself, and that always makes others more comfortable. It creates a sense of intimacy between preacher and people. And it enables those who are also hoarders in one way or another to identify with the preacher as they both stand under the judgment of the text.

6. *The piquant introduction.* I use this term to cover a broad range of introductions that have as their primary feature some story or remark so revelatory of human nature that it makes people smile to themselves and shake their heads in affirmation. Other kinds of introductions already listed can be piquant, too, but in this category I place all of those beginnings that do not seem to belong to other groupings or that have such a special piquancy that they deserve a category by themselves. Two examples will serve for clarification. When Robert McCracken was at Riverside Church, he preached a sermon on "The Wish to Escape." He discovered his introduction in a clipping from the *New York Times*. It told that a certain bus driver, sixteen years in the employment of his company, took the wheel of his bus and instead of piloting it back and forth on the streets of the Bronx as he had done every day, week in and week out, for all those years, drove it right down to Florida. McCracken announced as his text Ps. 55:6, "O for the wings of a dove that I might fly away and be at rest," related the escapade of the bus driver, and was on his way with the sermon. People chuckled at the incident and could relate to it. They too had had such impulses. As McCracken said, it was one of the most perfect introductions he had ever happened upon.[13]

The other example is from a sermon by Gene Bartlett on the parable of the prodigal son, called "The Long Way Home." The thrust of the sermon is about realizing our nature and God's nature — and how the prodigal had to go through the far country to discover the truth about himself and his father. Here is the piquant beginning:

> It is related that one day when G. K. Chesterton was packing his bags in his London apartment a friend came in and asked where he was going. Chesterton surprisingly replied that he was on his way to London. Somewhat taken back by this answer, the other countered that it might be in order to remind Chesterton that he already was in London. To this, however, the essayist replied with a characteristic twist. "No," he said, "that's where you're wrong. I no longer see London. Familiarity has closed my eyes. The real meaning of travel is to come home again and see it as though for the first time. So I really *am* on my way to London though I'll go by Paris, Rome, and Dresden."[14]

7. *The problem-centered introduction.* The sermon that deals with a particular problem faced by persons in the congregation may begin with any kind of introduction, but more often than not it will begin with an introduction that is itself focused on the problem to be faced in the body of the sermon. Here is such an introduction from Edmund Steimle's sermon "The Peril of Ordinary Days":

> One of life's commonest experiences is the letdown. After peak days like a graduation, a wedding, or a promotion come the humdrum ordinary days again with the inevitable letdown. Some people seem to have considerable difficulty accepting this fact of human experience. They refuse to adjust themselves to it and consequently live miserable lives while yearning for hours of excitement in which they can take the center of the stage and bask in the glory of it.
>
> Now this same fact of human experience is a part of man's religious life too. In the life journey of the soul there are luminous moments of inspiration when God seems near and real. But those moments are always followed by a letdown. And if you are ever going to be tempted to lose faith in God, nine times out of ten it will not be in moments of crisis when action or unusual courage is demanded, but rather in periods which the mystics call the "dry periods"—the days when nothing much happens and God seems far away and unreal. That is the peril of ordinary days because it is then that it is the easiest thing in the world to lose faith in God.[15]

The secret of the problem-centered introduction is to get as quickly as possible into the heart of the problem to be dealt with without seeming either cold and clinical or irrelevant and uninteresting. People need to identify with the problem being discussed, and therefore there must be an abundant sense of humanity in the preacher as he or she approaches it. I have found it effective, in my own problem-centered introductions, to cite the case of someone who has faced the particular problem, so that others may identify with a real instance of their problem and not a mere theoretical beginning. This, for example, is the introduction to a sermon called "Love Beyond the Grave," in which I tried to deal with the questions people have about relationships between the living and the dead:

I had a letter from a woman in northern Virginia. Her father had died, and she told me how much she missed him. He had been an exceptionally loving parent and had raised his children to enjoy life and to share their experiences in the family. When he died it tore a big hole in the fabric of the woman's life. "I am grateful for my memories," she said, "and I am not complaining about God's letting him die. But there is one thing I cannot understand. We have always been taught that love is the essence of our faith. How can that love be cut off by death?" She wanted an assurance that her father could still see her and be involved in her life — that death had not completely dissolved their beautiful relationship.

I understood what she meant. There is nothing harder to bear than the death of someone we love. During the early stages of grief, the heaviness can be almost unbearable. Even a great saint like C. S. Lewis was staggered by it when his wife died. He felt, he said, as if he were drunk or "concussed" — as if there were a blanket between him and the world. And the worst thing of all was that he couldn't pray. Every time he tried, it was as if a door shut in his face and he heard it being bolted on the other side.

This was what the woman was experiencing — the raw finality of death — the emptiness that comes with the loss. What could I say to her?

The creative preacher will use many forms of introduction in a lifetime and will vary them frequently so that people do not find them routine and monotonous. As R. E. O. White says in *A Guide to Preaching*: "Introductions fail if they are too predictable. Some men *always* begin with the context, or with a problem, or by arguing with some recent public statement, or by mentioning the name of the book that prompted the theme. As soon as the text is announced, or even the hymn before the sermon, habitual listeners can foresee how the preacher will begin: 'Not that again!' is a devastating comment. Our people will often grow fond of our mannerisms: but never of our lazy-mindedness."[16]

COMING TO AN END

"Other poets," said Herman Melville when speaking of whales and describing the enormous power and value of their tails, "have warbled the praises of the soft eye of the antelope, and the lovely plumage of the bird that never alights; less celestial, I celebrate a tail."[17] The conclusion of a sermon may seem less celestial than other parts, but it is no less important. A sermon without a fitting end is as unfinished and, in some ways, as powerless as a whale without a tail.

The conclusion of the sermon is, after all, the last moment you have with the congregation, the final opportunity to drive home some everlasting truth, to lift up some winsome ideal, to engage their wills in the performance of some sacred duty. It is the time when you complete Switzer's circle of requirements (see page 36) and lead the people to move from facing their situations, considering the alternatives, and deciding on a course of action to committing themselves to following that very course. To pull your punch at this point of the sermon and let the message simply fizzle out is to cancel the effectiveness of much that has gone before. It is like making an exciting ninety-yard run on the football field, twisting and turning and sidestepping opponents, only to trip over a shoelace and fumble the ball before reaching the goal line.

Great care should be taken, therefore, in the preparation of the final remarks of the sermon. The same thoughtfulness should go into the conclusion that has gone into the other parts. The ending should really conclude the sermon, should draw it to an appropriate close, so that people know, psychologically and aesthetically, it is finished. "Many sermons leave an impression like the delta of the

Mississippi," said Henry Sloane Coffin. "They sprawl away, instead of coming to a clear destination."[18] We do not wish to sprawl away in our endings. People should have the same satisfaction when the last word is spoken that playgoers had when seeing the conclusion of a play by Sophocles, which is to say, a feeling of the inevitability of it all and of their need to respond with their very lives.

It is unfortunate, as George Sweazey has observed, that the conclusion of the sermon is burdened with two handicaps: "The minister prepares it when he is the most tired, and the congregation hears it when they are the most tired."[19] But both problems are easily met. The minister simply prepares the conclusion — or at least the essence of it — when preparing the outline of the entire sermon. That way it does not become the victim of mental fatigue. And the congregation, if the sermon has been well crafted and well delivered from beginning to end, will have no difficulty in listening to the conclusion. The crowd at a ball game is never too tired to witness the exciting finish to a closely fought game. The audience in a theater is not thinking about personal comfort as a gripping play reaches its denouement. It is only when the ending is sloppy, or when it follows a poorly conceived and badly executed sermon, that we have any cause for uneasiness.

WAYS OF CONCLUDING

There are numerous ways of drawing the sermon to a close. Much depends on the sensibilities of the preacher. He or she has designed the sermon from a personal viewpoint and will have certain feelings about the natural way to end it. There will be force lines, filaments, organic relationships to consider. Otherwise the ending would seem forced or inappropriate, like a stock remark that takes no account of the flow of conversation.

There are, however, a few rather standard methods of concluding the sermon. They are provided here for the purpose of analysis, not in order to recommend one above another.

1. *Letting the last point serve as an ending.* This method was often used by Phillips Brooks. It is especially appropriate for sermons organized according to the "faceting" technique described on pages 55–57. In general, it is not a good idea to introduce new

material into the conclusion of a sermon, for this interrupts the process of "winding down" in the minds of the congregation. In the faceting sermon, however, the major thrust of the sermon — the primary facet — has been given early on, and the other points have been ancillary to that. Therefore the new material does not have the kind of impact that new material has in a developmental sermon; it is not of an ascending character, rising in interest above what has already been said. The last point thus carries us but a bit farther along the general emphasis of the sermon and can, if well chosen, help in a practical way to implement the truth of the previous parts of the sermon.

This can be seen in the final point or conclusion of Brooks's sermon "Standing Before God," which was outlined on page 56. The point is: We need not be dead to stand before God; that wonderful experience can begin now.

And now one question still remains! Is the fulfillment of the vision of St. John for any man to wait until that man is dead? Can only the dead stand before God? Think for a moment what we found to be the blessings of that standing before God, and then consider that those privileges, however they may be capable of being given more richly to the soul of man in the eternal world, are privileges upon whose enjoyment any man's soul may enter here. Consider this, and the question is at once answered. . . . Is it not true . . . that Christ does for the soul which follows him, that which the experience of the eternal world shall take up and certify, and complete? Already in Him we begin to live the everlasting life. Already its noble independence, its deep discrimination, its generous charity, its large hopefulness, its great abounding and inspiring peace gathers around and fills the soul which lives in obedience to Him. Already, as He himself said, "He that believeth on the Son hath everlasting life."

And yet, while we need not wait till we are dead for the privilege and power of "standing before God," yet still the knowledge of that loftier and more manifest standing before Him, which is to come in the unseen land, of which St. John has told us, may make more possible the true experience of the divine presence which we may have here. Because I am to stand before Him in some yet unimagined way, seeing Him with some keener sight, hearing His words with some quicker hearing which shall belong to some new condition of eternity, therefore I will be sure that my true life here consists in such a degree of realization of His presence, such a standing before

94

Him in obedience, and faith, and love, as is possible for one in this lower life.

When the change comes to any of us, my friends, how little it will be, if we have really been, through the power of Jesus Christ, standing before God, in our poor, half-blind way upon the earth. If now, in the bright freshness of your youth, you give yourself to Christ, and through him do indeed know God as your dearest friend, years and years hence, when the curtain is drawn back for you, and you are bidden to join the host of the dead who stand before God eternally, how slight the change will be. Only the change from the struggle to the victory, only the opening of the dusk and twilight into the perfect day. "Well done, good and faithful servant, thou hast been faithful over a few things. Enter thou into the joy of thy Lord."[20]

What conclusion could be more fitting than this for a sermon on standing before God? Yet, as can be seen from the outline on page 57, this is a new point in the sermon. It has not really been touched on before.

2. *Summarizing what has been said.* There is value, especially in sermons that have been analytical or argumentative, in recapitulation. As the old folk preacher said: "First, I tells 'em what I'm gonna tell 'em. Next, I tells 'em. And, then, I tells 'em what I tol' 'em." This approach often gives added clarity to a sermon. I once preached a "teaching" sermon on "The Worship of God." The sermon began with an allusion to Karl Barth's description of a scene in a certain monastery in Alsace. While the monks were chanting the Magnificat, a French shell suddenly tore through the roof and exploded in the nave of the church. When the smoke and dust had cleared, the monks were still there, chanting the Magnificat. What is the compelling nature of worship, I asked, that would account for such remarkable devotion? Beginning with the simplest definition of worship, as recognizing the worth or value of something, I used the body of the sermon to explore the meaning and nature of the worship of God. The conclusion then became an occasion for summarizing what I had said and tying the ending to the beginning:

What is the nature of worship? Let us see if we cannot form an answer now. The recognition of the absolute worthiness of God, and

95

of man's total dependence upon Him for all things, both in the acts and mysteries of life, constitutes the beginning of worship for any of us; the life lived in joyous commitment to his glory and worthship constitutes its middle; and the devout approach to death as a glad renunciation of this world, in order more fully to participate in that glory and worthship, is its final consummation. We are God's, shaped of his earth unto his ends, and the chief joy of our mortal being is the discovery of our immortal relationship to him.

Knowing this, a man might well stand at the altar though the shells burst about him.[21]

3. *Concluding with an illustration.* The aim of any sermon is to help people to embody some truth or insight in their own living. It often seems helpful, therefore, to conclude the sermon with a brief narrative or illustration showing how the ideas of the sermon can be given shape in a real situation. This method is a favorite of evangelists, for it has a way of catching up the will of the hearer and moving it beyond the hesitancies of the analytical mind. The responsible preacher will take care not to abuse the technique by imposing unfairly on people's emotions. But used properly, it is an effective and significant way of ending the sermon. People can often remember a picture better than they can remember an idea, and concluding with an illustration impresses them with an image that will keep the sermon alive for a long time.

J. Wallace Hamilton preached a sermon on the text, "Jesus said unto him, If thou wilt be perfect, go and sell that thou hast, and give to the poor, and thou shalt have treasure in heaven: and come and follow me" (Matt. 19:21). The title of the sermon was "The World Is Not Enough." The thrust of the sermon had to do with renouncing worldly success in favor of heavenly treasures. Here is the conclusion Hamilton gave:

When I came from Canada to this country I was very young. My sister, who came with me, was younger still. We were both as green as the country fields where, up to then, we had lived. We had heard a lot about Chicago—that awful, wicked city where gangsters lie in wait in dark alleys, and all eight-year-olds carry guns—and when we reached Chicago and walked out of the station into the roaring street, I kept my hand on my watch. . . . We were afraid to take a taxi from the station; we had heard that smart taxi-drivers would take country folk like us ten miles around the city in order to reach an address two blocks from the station. . . . So we lugged our heavy luggage aboard a streetcar. I handed the conductor a quarter — a perfectly good *Canadian* quarter; he handed it back, saying gruffly, "Counterfeit!" Something not quite Christian rose in me, and I felt like telling him something, but the crowd behind us was pushing to get on, so we scrambled off, luggage, quarter, and all — including our anger. Just for that, we wouldn't ride on his old streetcar, at any price. We lugged our heavy grips for twenty city blocks. I never did find out whether or not the city of Chicago was disappointed at losing our patronage that day, but the next day we exchanged our Canadian money for currency acceptable in the new country.

Do you see what I am driving at? We shall all shortly be moving to a new country — a country of the spirit, where there is nothing but spirit. *We had better become acquainted at the spiritual bank!*[22]

4. *Concluding with a quotation.* This was once a favorite way of ending a sermon. Preachers kept omnibus volumes of poetry, hymns, and stirring quotations that they ransacked for appropriate endings to their homilies. The method is not widely used now, for several reasons. People are not oriented today toward poetic expression, and recitation does not enjoy the favor it once did as a form of entertainment. The new poetry does not lend itself to declamation as the old did; its rhythms are irregular, and it seldom rhymes. Therefore it is neither easy to memorize nor easy to understand when heard. But a few poignant lines or a well-put verse of a hymn can still be quite effective if the preacher speaks them clearly and they echo or enlarge upon some salient point of a sermon. It is probably wise not to attempt too long a quotation or to use the method very frequently. And it may be helpful to include the passage verbatim in the worship bulletin, so that people may take it away with them and ponder it, or even memorize it, in their homes; that way the sermon is given extended life in their daily affairs.

5. *Concluding with the text.* Sometimes there is nothing more apt for closing a sermon than the text with which the sermon began. The preacher, instead of dealing immediately with the text, may choose to begin with an idea or a problem and work gradually toward the text, culminating the sermon with it. This is precisely what Deryl Fleming, minister of the Ravensworth Bap-

tist Church in Annandale, Virginia, did in a sermon called "When
the Other Person's Grass Looks Greener." Fleming began the
sermon by recalling a cartoon that gave an aerial view of a field
divided by fences into four quadrants. There was a cow in each
section of the field, and each was sticking its neck through the
fence, eating grass from the next section. The sermon dealt with
the human tendency to envy others and wish to have what they
have. The antidote to the anxiety produced by this, suggested
Fleming, is to experience the love of God in such a way that one
no longer envies others, but wishes to share with them. The conclusion of the sermon then embodies the text which had been in
the preacher's mind from the beginning:

> The psalmist confesses that he was almost done for, about to despair
> of his plight and settle down in envy and resentment. Then he went
> into the sanctuary and regained his perspective. He saw the end of
> lives posited on false values. He envisioned the sufficiency of God's
> loving presence with and provision for him:
> When my soul was embittered, when I was pricked in heart,
> I was stupid and ignorant, I was like a beast toward thee.
> Nevertheless I am continually with thee; thou dost hold my
>   right hand.
> Thou dost guide me with thy counsel, and afterward thou wilt
>   receive me to glory.
> Whom have I in heaven but thee? And there is nothing upon earth
>   that I desire besides thee.
> My flesh and my heart may fail, but God is the strength of my heart
>   and my portion for ever.
> Psalm 73:21–26
> With that perspective of God and of oneself, the other person's grass
> no longer looks greener, and one's own life begins the process of
> greening.

6. *Simply following through the lines of force begun in the
sermon.* This is probably the most frequently used way of ending
a sermon. It is like the follow-through of a golfer's swing; the trick
is to let yourself feel the natural movement of the sermon and
pursue the movement to its own inevitable conclusion. The
method requires sensitivity. You must really listen to the sermon
and be in tune to where it is going. Occasionally it will require

ending the sermon in a way you had not intended when you made the outline. Everything depends on the inner motion of the sermon, the momentum that has been building as the sermon was written. Done well, this is one of the most effective ways to conclude. The congregation feels satisfied, as if it has had a good meal and ended it with a cup of rich coffee and a keen-tasting mint, savored slowly and deliberately, without the suggestion of rushing to be through.

Here is the conclusion I gave to a sermon entitled "The Great Importance of Little Deeds":

> It's an exciting thought, isn't it, that when we die and come into the presence of God in all its fullness, it will not be our major achievements that speak for us—"He was president of a bank," "She was the first woman senator from her state," "He was the author of twenty-two books"—but the small, apparently inconsequential things we long ago forgot: "He mowed my lawn when I was sick," "She cared for my child while I went to the market," "He sent me flowers when I needed them most," "She washed and mended my socks." These are the little things that hold the world together. They are the small stones that comprise the great cathedrals where God is worshiped. And they shall be remembered like stars in the crowns of all the saints.

These are not summary remarks, neither are they entirely new at the end of the sermon. They grow naturally out of the filaments of the sermon; only now the filaments are winding together and closing, bringing everything to an end.

7. *Ending with no ending.* This is a semantical trick, of course. To conclude with words to the effect that there is no real ending to the sermon is to make a kind of ending, whatever one says. But occasionally the preacher may wish to employ this technique as a way of breaking off the sermon at the particular time in the liturgy but allowing it to continue to work itself out in the thinking and lives of the congregation. George Buttrick gave a "no ending" conclusion to his sermon "Who Owns the Earth?" based on Ps. 24:1, "The earth is the Lord's." He said:

> There is no conclusion to this sermon. Perhaps there never should be any for any sermon, for hearer and preacher alike must write the

conclusion, each in his own secret commitment, each in his daily life in the earth which God owns. Suppose Christian Dior and his successors never did own any fashions! Wouldn't that be a revolution? Suppose the money in our pocket was never ours, and suppose the banker never owned the bank! What a change, if we knew it, in our acquisitive society! So each of us writes a conclusion as he may be minded. But perhaps our minds also are not ours. The Bible in its vast ponderings goes far beyond "the earth." It says "The earth is the Lord's and the fulness thereof," meaning everything in the cosmos; "the world and those who dwell therein," meaning you and me, and the whole pilgrimage of man, and all other orders of life. "For he has founded it upon the seas, and established it upon the rivers": it all rests on the Abyss of His eternal nature and is all held in His eternal grace.[23]

In literature this device is known as *occupatio* — denying that one is doing something while in the very act of doing it. But it can be very effective, as this passage from Buttrick shows, as a way of ending the sermon.

SOME GENERAL COMMENTS

How long should the ending be? Some preachers say it should be very brief — a mere flourish at the end. Others say it should be longer — long enough to drive the nails that have been started in the sermon and then to lay the hammer down. Both are right. The length must be allowed to vary, depending on the style of the sermon and the lines of force in it. Sometimes the lines will carry the ending on for quite a way; at other times they will permit it to stop in a short distance. One can no more mandate the length of conclusions for all sermons than one can say that the length of tails of all the beasts in the jungle should be precisely twelve inches.

What is important is that the conclusion be suited to the sermon. Just as an introduction ought to introduce a particular sermon, and not serve as well to introduce half a dozen sermons, the ending ought to belong to the sermon it concludes. One proof that it does is the way the preacher is able to relate it to the introduction, thus tying up the sermon into a neat whole. If the introduction raised a question, the conclusion may allude to the question and to the answer that has been found. If the introduction stated a problem, the conclusion may, in a word or a phrase, refer again to the problem while summarizing the solution. Often it is merely a rhetorical achievement. The echoing of a phrase or a sentence serves to unite the beginning and the ending. But it says that the preacher knew where he or she was going and has been in control of the material of the sermon.

In my sermon "There Is Still God," for example, I began with a reference to my twelve-year-old son's budding agnosticism and to Lorraine Hansberry's play *A Raisin in the Sun* in which Mama, the head of a black household in Chicago's South Side, deals with an agnostic daughter by making her repeat, "In my mother's house there is still God." In the body of the sermon, I appealed to the evidences for God's existence in two major areas of life—our pains and our joys—neither of which can be fully understood apart from God. I moved quickly from the second area to the conclusion:

> I can't explain it without God. Sometimes when I am too busy, or when things are going too smoothly for me, I don't think about him. I don't bow my head and say "Thank you," or stop what I am doing and say "You," as if he had surprised me again. But when there is pain, I think of him, and when there is joy, I remember. Whenever I get off dead center of myself, I see him, and know that he sustains the world I live in, the real world, the world beyond the world of my comfort and forgetfulness.
>
> Then I understand a remark which Tom Stoppard put into his play *Jumpers*, that atheism is only "a crutch for those who cannot bear the reality of God." And I remember why the medieval philosophers called him the *ens realissimum*, the "most real thing there is." And I recall St. Paul's way of putting it, that "in him we live and move, in him we exist"—*esmen*, in the Greek—"in him we live and move and ARE."
>
> And I say, THERE IS STILL GOD IN THIS HOUSE.

The repetition of the phrase in the final moments of the sermon reinforces it in the minds of the hearers, so that they will carry it away and remember the sermon by it.

William Wand, the bishop of London, put it this way in *Letters on Preaching*: "It always gives a congregation a happy feeling to find a preacher ending up where he began. The reminiscence of his opening theme may be marked by the repetition of a phrase, or suggested by the overtones of a single word, used in the beginning; or it may be conveyed by a brief sentence summing up the whole argument, or even by the mere iteration of his text. In any case the congregation is not only reminded of the main point he has been trying to emphasize, but he also has the comforting assurance that he knew all the time what he wanted to say and that he has triumphantly brought to conclusion a well-thought-out plan. Such treatment produces a feeling of confidence towards the preacher, which may turn out valuable in many other departments of parochial and pastoral life."[24]

The conclusion of the sermon, then, coming at the rear of everything, is not so humble an artifice as it might at first appear, and we might well, having "warbled the praises" of the introduction, in Melville's words, learn now to "celebrate a tail."

NOTES

1. W. E. Sangster, *The Craft of Sermon Construction* (Philadelphia: Westminster Press, 1951), p. 136.

2. J. Randall Nichols, *Building the Word: The Dynamics of Communication and Preaching* (New York: Harper & Row, 1980), pp. 101–3.

3. Robert J. McCracken, *The Making of the Sermon* (New York: Harper & Brothers, 1956), p. 91.

4. Sangster, *The Craft of Sermon Construction*, pp. 134–35.

5. John R. Fry, *Fire and Blackstone* (Philadelphia: J. B. Lippincott, 1969), pp. 85–93.

6. George A. Buttrick, *Sermons Preached in a University Church* (Nashville: Abingdon Press, 1959), p. 13.

7. Edmund A. Steimle, *From Death to Birth* (Philadelphia: Fortress Press, 1973), p. 115.

8. Leslie Weatherhead, *Key Next Door* (London: Hodder & Stoughton, 1959), p. 3.

9. Herbert H. Farmer, *The Healing Cross* (London: Nisbet and Co., 1938), pp. 65–66.

10. David H. C. Read, *Religion Without Wrappings* (Grand Rapids: Wm. B. Eerdmans Publishing Co., 1970), pp. 159–160.

11. J. Wallace Hamilton, *Ride the Wild Horses! The Christian Use of Our Untamed Impulses* (Westwood, N.J.: Fleming H. Revell Co., 1952), p. 26.

12. Robert Raines, *To Kiss the Joy* (Waco, Tex.: Word Books, 1973), pp. 30–33.

13. McCracken, *The Making of a Sermon*, p. 92.

14. In G. Paul Butler, ed., *Best Sermons, 1962* (Princeton: D. Van Nostrand Co., 1962), p. 82.

15. Edmund A. Steimle, *Are You Looking for God?* (Philadelphia: Fortress Press, 1957), p. 41.

16. R. E. O. White, *A Guide to Preaching* (Grand Rapids: Wm. B. Eerdmans Publishing Co., 1973), p. 117.

17. Herman Melville, *Moby Dick* (New York: Modern Library, 1950), p. 372.

18. Donald Macleod, ed., *Here Is My Method: The Art of Sermon Construction* (Westwood, N.J.: Fleming H. Revell Co., 1952), p. 57.

19. George Sweazey, *Preaching the Good News* (Englewood Cliffs, N.J.: Prentice-Hall, 1976), p. 100.

20. Phillips Brooks, *Twenty Sermons* (New York: E. P. Dutton & Co., 1903), pp. 73–75.

21. John Killinger, *The Thickness of Glory* (Nashville: Abingdon Press, 1965), p. 77.

22. Hamilton, *Ride the Wild Horses!* pp. 63–64.

23. Buttrick, *Sermons Preached in a University Church*, p. 95.

24. William Wand, *Letters on Preaching* (London: Hodder & Stoughton, 1974), p. 45.

---6---

Illustrating the
Sermon

The Bible is rich in imagery. This fact, more than any other, has
kept it alive through the centuries. People remember its pictures—the Garden of Eden, the burning bush, the exodus, the
tablets of the law, the Temple of Solomon, the exile, the crucifixion, the empty tomb, Pentecost, the Holy City—and their lives are
strengthened and changed by these images. They remember the
stories—Adam and Eve hiding from God, David killing a giant,
Hosea reclaiming an unfaithful wife, Peter denying his Master, a
loving father receiving his prodigal son—and live out their own
stories through the biblical paradigms. It would be impossible to
imagine the Judeo-Christian faith without images.

By the same token, it is hard to imagine Christian preaching
without the power and beauty of images—both those from the
Bible and those from the preacher's own experiences, added to give
current depth and clarification to the message. Image-making and
storytelling are part of the faith. The faith continues to generate
them. To say, as Geoffrey W. Bromiley has, "I am not very fond
of illustrations, except from the Bible, largely because I often find
that they are remembered when the points illustrated are forgotten,"[1] is to misunderstand not only the art of effective communication but the nature of the faith itself. The heart of Christianity is
the incarnation—God taking flesh in our midst—truth taking a
body and a local habitation, with all the risks and liabilities
involved. Preaching is also incarnation—putting ideas and theological abstractions into warm and living pictures, with all the

danger involved in that. The Gospel of Luke, someone has figured, is 52 percent parable. Imagine how much poorer our tradition would be if Luke had been afraid of illustrations! Our faith is much more than proposition. It is a way of seeing — of imagining how things ought to be. It cannot be confined to bare statements.

We now know, through modern research on the brain, that there are two hemispheres of mental activity, each with a unique capacity. The left side of the brain, which controls the right side of the body, is pragmatic and analytical. The right side, which controls the alternate side of the body, is meditative and imagistic. Some persons have developed the capacities of one side more than the other. Professors, mathematicians, physicists, engineers, are often left-brained; they think in abstractions and formulas. Artists, poets, film-makers, designers, tend to be right-brained; they apprehend the world through images and metaphors. To be whole, a person needs to develop both sides of the brain. Then the person can function rationally when rationality is most useful and intuitively when the other nature is called for.

The imbalance in the way most people use their brains probably accounts for the fact that some preachers are more abstract and propositional in their preaching, while others tend to be storytellers and illustrators. Some are like Euclid, who Edna St. Vincent Millay said "looked on Beauty bare" — they see truth naked and unadorned, in all its logical purity. Others are like Michelangelo, who put all his theology into the silent glory of the Sistine Chapel.

The same phenomenon, too, surely accounts for the way people "hear" sermons. Some persons, being naturally given to logic and abstraction, listen intently to sermons that are well thought out, lucidly argued, and plainly delivered. I have in mind a certain doctor, a surgeon, who is enraptured by such sermons; they have the kind of precision he adores. Other persons, less used to thinking about difficult matters, find abstract sermons boring to the nth degree. They much prefer parables and stories — pictures of life they can "see" with their minds.

A good sermon usually achieves a healthy balance between abstraction and imagery. It is well conceived and clearly stated for those who need to receive the truth propositionally; and it is also well illustrated for those whose mode of reception is more pictorial. The Bible has this kind of balance about it. It is image and story, as we have said, but it is also law and history and proverb and philosophy. It alternates between these, so that story is always given a rational "spine" and statement is always provided a nearby illustration.

The competent preacher, therefore, will make a sound and substantial outline of the sermon, testing it for logic and theological meaning. Then he or she will consult the right side of the brain for ways of illustrating the thoughts, of turning them into images or pictures that will give them life and specificity. Gordon W. Ireson in *How Shall They Hear?* recommends a habit which he follows:

> I have myself made it a systematic practice for years to supply my own illustrations when reading a theological book. Suppose I were trying to teach this truth to others: how would I illustrate it? What is the point or principle involved? What is analogous to it in everyday experience? It has been an exacting but immensely profitable discipline. If I can't produce an illustration, it is because I haven't properly understood the point at issue.[2]

The preacher, in similar fashion, studies the outline of the sermon and asks: How can I illustrate this? What experience have people had that would help them to grasp it? What picture can I give that will clarify it and help them to remember it?

One is forced to judge, from the response people make to those who preach in stories and pictures, that the majority of persons in any congregation "hear" better with the right side of the brain than with the left. Jesus apparently experienced this in his day; he gave his disciples his teachings in propositional form, but usually taught the masses in parables. The preacher can refuse to submit to the way things are — can abjure sermon illustrations as common or lowbrow ("Christian cartoons," one seminary student called them). But the preacher who really cares about communicating a message will learn to use them and use them well. We shall not redeem the world from irresponsible evangelists by eschewing their art of storytelling. It is far better to learn their art and beat

106

them at the game by preaching popular sermons whose grammar and theology are *correct*!

WHAT ILLUSTRATIONS DO
FOR THE SERMON

Some preachers have a knack for illustrating sermons. They think pictorially. Their very language is rich in imagery and metaphor. Others have a difficult time with illustrations. Their thought is more prosaic. Sometimes they feel the way Charles Duthie, the Scottish preacher, did:

> I am not fond of accumulating vivid illustrations. Perhaps I am defective in imagination but I have come to feel that the cult of the illustration has been overdone and that the primary need of our time is the need for fundamental spiritual principles, clearly and vigorously presented. An illustration may be a window that lets in the light but a good sermon must have more in it than glass![3]

Duthie is right, a good sermon must have more than glass. But must it be a warehouse, devoid of any natural illumination at all? Perhaps what is needed is an understanding of exactly what it is that illustrations do for a sermon. Then, when we know their proper function, we can use them to enhance the sermon, and not as a substitute for vigorous thinking.

1. *Illustrations help to make the sermon clear.* We must always remember in preaching that people cannot follow our thoughts as easily as they read a newspaper or a novel. When something is not clear as they read, they can return to the sentence, linger over it, and usually come up with the sense of it before proceeding to the next sentence. Not so when they are listening to us! The moving tongue speaks, to paraphrase the *Rubaiyat*, and, having spoken, moves on. There is no time to ponder. A good speaker watches the audience for signs of difficulty in comprehension and tries to adjust his or her pace to the level of response. Even so, some people will lose the thread of thought and be unable to follow. Illustrations are enormously helpful in clarifying meaning. The thoughtful preacher uses them especially at the points of the sermon where

there is likely to be confusion or lack of understanding. They not only provide momentary surcease in the flow of the sermon, so people can linger over the ideas, but bring illumination to the ideas. An illustration, as Ian Macpherson says, is "the spark that flashes out so brilliantly that what is seen can never be forgotten."[4]

2. *Illustrations make the sermon interesting.* This is not to suggest that ideas are not interesting in and of themselves. The sermons of Gossip and Scherer and Buttrick had a glow about them in all their parts. But anecdotes, stories, and piquant remarks have a color that is hard to match in the more prosaic sections of a sermon. Everybody loves a story. People in groups invariably brighten when someone begins to tell a tale. And congregations are no exception. Their response level immediately leaps forward when the preacher starts an illustration.

3. *Illustrations relate theology to life.* As Sangster says, they "earth" a sermon. They take it out of the realm of abstraction and anchor it to everyday occurrences, to the things people know. William James and John Dewey wanted a philosophy that could wear overalls. Illustrations are where the sermon puts on its overalls and goes to work in people's lives. The people in the congregation know in the illustrations whether the sermon is practical or not; if they can see the principles at work in the stories, then they know the principles will work for them. Many times they recall the theological implications of the stories when they can't recall the theology itself.

4. *Illustrations "rest" the congregation.* Listening intently is hard work. It requires great concentration, especially if the material being listened to is very tightly argued. The use of an illustration in the midst of a sermon permits people to relax for a few moments and listen less intently. We said earlier that the development of a sermon can be compared to the development of an Elizabethan play; the intensity of the experience builds and builds until a climax is reached and there is a slight diminution of excitement before the end. It was also observed that the great tragedian Shakespeare often used comic relief as a means of relaxing the audience before carrying it further toward the climax. Illustrations serve a similar purpose in the sermon. They let the congrega-

tion breathe more easily before plunging back into the thought line of the sermon. An observant preacher can see it happen when he or she begins an illustration: people begin to breathe more deeply and readjust themselves in their seats. Then, as the sermon moves on, they become tense again, trying to follow the train of thought. A sermon without these "rest stops" can seem very long and tedious.

5. *Illustrations intensify the emotional level of a sermon.* This may appear to be a contradiction to what has just been said about illustrations relaxing people. But there are two facets to every listener, one intellectual and the other emotional. The thought substance of the sermon challenges people's intellectual attention; it is from this that illustrations provide temporary relief. The illustrations, on the other hand, often have a great effect on people's emotional levels. Because the illustrations carry the "incarnate" aspect of thought and relate theology to life, they are more likely to stimulate people's feelings about things. This is why all the great evangelists of history have been storytellers. They have used illustrations to develop emotional intensity until people could no longer resist the call to the Christian life. The preacher must be careful not to use the power of stories unduly to manipulate a congregation and cause people to do things they would not ordinarily do. But any preacher who wishes to lead a congregation to new convictions for living will do well to study the art of illustrating sermons.

6. *Illustrations help make a sermon memorable.* Ask any child who has come from church on Sunday to recount the sermon and the child will probably remember an illustration. The same is true of adults. We remember stories and illustrative remarks. If they embody the truths of a sermon, the sermon will be much easier to recall than if it were merely propositional in nature. Often people can recall a sermon years later on the basis of the illustrations in it. They will say, "Do you remember that sermon you preached that had a story about a tiger in it?" Or, "I still think about that sermon that had the missionary touching the face of a leper and saying to himself, 'Well, God, this is it, I can't go back now.'" We don't forget word pictures the way we do ordinary words. Even the

preacher remembers the illustrations better, both at the time of preaching the sermon and later when trying to recall it.

THE KINDS OF ILLUSTRATIONS

Thoughtful preachers usually attempt to adjust their illustrating of sermons to the nature of their hearers. Henry Ward Beecher said that if he looked into the congregation and saw a sailor, he immediately began to think of seafaring illustrations that would help him make his point. George Buttrick, when he was at Madison Avenue Presbyterian Church in New York, bore in mind the various professions represented in his congregation on a given Sunday and tried frequently to use illustrations that would appeal to doctors, lawyers, and corporate executives, who were always present in large numbers. When he went to Harvard University as dean of the chapel, his sermons became sprinkled with references to contemporary poets and scientists. Bryant Kirkland of Fifth Avenue Presbyterian Church in New York says that he makes a conscious effort to relate illustrations to age groups. "When I use something that expresses the youth culture," he says, "I can see the kids' eyes light up; then when I turn to something about the golden years, I see the old folks' eyes light up."

There are many ways of classifying illustrations — by professions, by age groupings, by topics, by sources. Most preachers seldom think of classifications. They simply think of illustrations that fit their needs in particular sermons. But it may help the beginning preacher if we take a partial look at the broad spectrum of the kinds of illustrations often used. The method of classification is purely arbitrary and serves only the purpose of exhibiting the scope of illustrative material.

1. *Biblical illustrations.* It is often possible to illustrate a truth by reference to some biblical character, event, or teaching. For example, a preacher talking about joy might refer to the song of Miriam in Exodus 15, which celebrated the escape of the Hebrews from slavery in Egypt. Or a preacher speaking of the way people use religion for their own selfish purposes could recall the time when Simon Magus approached the apostles and tried to buy the

power of the Holy Spirit in order to become a more powerful sorcerer (Acts 8:18–19). The Bible is a great treasury of illustrative material, and an additional advantage to using it in this way is that it acquaints people with biblical material they have either forgotten or never known, producing a more biblically literate community.

2. *Historical illustrations.* The minister who knows history well is at a great advantage when it comes to illustrating sermons. In every sermon, happenings from the past will leap at him or her to illumine some contemporary emphasis. John Sutherland Bonnell was preaching an Easter sermon on the text, "Thanks be to God, which giveth us the victory through our Lord Jesus Christ" (1 Cor. 15:57). He wished to refute those who believe that civilization is on an upward march that will one day achieve victory without God. "When an atomic bomb burst over Hiroshima," he said, "it destroyed not merely a populous city, but also shattered forever the notion of the inevitability of human progress." Bonnell continued:

> In the fifth century of the Christian era, Alaric, with his hordes of Visigoths, swept across Italy and finally captured Rome. The mistress of the world had fallen before the barbarians. Reading the history of the time, one can almost hear the crash of a falling empire and the crackle of leaping flames.
>
> Augustine, who lived through this experience, writes: "Horrible things have been told us. There have been ruins and fires and rapine and murder and torture. This is true. We have heard it many times. We have shuddered at all this disaster. We have wept and we have hardly been able to console ourselves."
>
> These words were penned at the beginning of the fifth century A.D. Fourteen hundred years have passed since that day, and Augustine's words could be reproduced as a description of our own time.[5]

3. *Biographical illustrations.* Biography has long been one of the greatest sources of sermon illustrations. Fosdick was so fond of illustrations from the lives of well-known persons that he read omnivorously in their biographies. It is almost impossible to read a good life study without discovering at least five or six usable vignettes or quotations. Here, for example, are some unadorned

passages from the autobiography of William Barclay, the great New Testament commentator:

> As I come near to the end of my days, the one thing that haunts me more than anything else is that I have been so unsatisfactory a husband and a father.[6]

> When I die, I should like to slip out of the room without fuss—for what matters is not what I am leaving, but where I am going.[7]

> She [Barclay's mother] died in 1932 of cancer of the spine, an agonizing death—and left me facing the theological problems that to this day I have never solved. Why should my mother, lovely in body and in spirit, good all through, have to die like that? She died just when I was being licensed as a preacher. "You'll have a new note in your preaching now," my father said to me through his own tears—and so I had—not the note of one who knew the answers and had solved the problems, but the note of one who now knew what the problems were.[8]

Any preacher who cannot sometime use these personal notes in a sermon is either ignorant or insensitive or both.

4. *Humorous illustrations.* By its very nature, humor often carries insights about life and living that are extremely useful in a sermon. Humor can come from many places—funny remarks, cartoons, comic strips, unusual experiences, even jokes. And humor is disarming. It slips up on our blind sides and reveals truths we weren't expecting. It deals effectively with sensitive issues, provided it does not make an opponent the butt of a joke. It simplifies complicated situations and makes an easier access to profound ideas. Suppose the preacher is preaching on the text in 2 Chron. 6:18, when Solomon has built the Temple: "But will God dwell indeed with man on the earth? Behold, heaven and the highest heaven cannot contain thee; how much less this house which I have built!" It is a mighty concept, but how plain it is made in a cartoon in *The Churchman* magazine. The cartoon shows a very small boy standing before a very large church door and asking the minister in the doorway, "Is God home?"[9] We can see immediately the impossibility of God's being confined to the church building.

5. *Scientific Illustrations.* Because we live in a technological era, it is important for the minister to translate biblical understandings

through illustrations from the various physical and life sciences: chemistry, physics, geology, cosmology, biology, psychology, sociology, medicine, and the like. It is a good idea to subscribe to at least one popular scientific journal and one popular psychological journal in order to keep abreast of developments and be able to find illustrative material in the various fields. Bryant Kirkland, in a sermon called "Look Fear in the Eye," wished to underline the deleterious effects of fear in persons' lives. He cited the following illustration:

There was an experiment at an upper New York state university called "The Sheep of Ithaca." The actions sound rather harsh but the experimenters gave electric shocks to sheep to see how much they could withstand. What resulted was that the sheep began to anticipate the next shock and became anxious as they waited for these intermittent irritations. Many of them died and the rest were disrupted by the anxiety of anticipation.[10]

6. *Geographical or topographical illustrations.* Preachers often find very dramatic and illuminative sermon illustrations as they travel from one region or country to another. Innumerable sermons have received support from descriptions of the sea, of various rivers, of mountains, of foreign cities and villages, and even of the heavens above these places.

James Stewart of Scotland concludes a great sermon called "Beyond Disillusionment to Faith" with the following words:

I remember once near Interlaken waiting for days to see the Jungfrau which was hidden in mists. People told me it was there, and I should have been a fool to doubt their word, for those who told me lived there and they knew. Then one day the mists were gone, and the whole great mountain stood revealed. Next day the mists were back, but now I had seen, and knew myself that it was true. Men and women, let us trust the saints, the people who have a right to speak about the fellowship of Christ, because they have lived in that country all their lives. Yes, and let us trust our own moments of vision: what matter if there are days when the mists come down and the face of God is hidden? We have seen, and we know for ever that this is real, so real that by it we can live and die. And if you are in Church one day, even if you have brought a clamouring crowd of doubts and worries and perplexities with you, do tell yourself: This is the abiding reality of life! I have seen it with the mists off, and I know. It was valid once, and it is valid now and for ever.[11]

Even if Stewart had not enjoyed the trip to Interlaken, with its beautiful vistas of lakes and mountains, it was worth going there for this single illustration!

7. *Poetic or rhetorical illustrations.* These are bits of poetry or prose chosen for the brightly glittering way they phrase a matter, so that they illustrate a point and make it memorable for people. It is best if they are kept brief, for people these days do not follow long quotations well. But quotations can turn an immense light on a subject in a very few moments. Consider these jewels for their powers of refraction:

> The Christian mystery is the darkness which makes light more plain.[12]
>
> God comprises, but is not, the universe.[13]
>
> Blessed be he who has saved a child's heart from despair![14]
>
> Lie here, beloved dust, until the joyful dawn.[15]

8. *Fictional illustrations.* Short stories and novels often provide superlative illustrative material for sermons. Experienced preachers know that they will find several helpful stories, remarks, or scenarios in books by Elie Wiesel, Leon Uris, Frederick Buechner, Kurt Vonnegut, Jr., Flannery O'Connor, John Irving, and other contemporary writers. An example of the effective way to employ such an illustration is in a sermon by Browne Barr called "The Soul's Invisible Jail." Barr's central thrust in the sermon is about the importance of forgiveness, and he has raised the question of how we are to forgive others. He recalls a scene in Erich Maria Remarque's novel *All Quiet on the Western Front*, which was based on real-life experiences the author had as a German soldier in World War I:

> The author describes an assault in which at one point, when they came in contact with the enemy, he leaped into a shell hole. In the shell hole he found an Englishman. After the first shock of fright he

114

considered what he should do now. Should they proceed to bayonet each other? But this bit of reflection was soon ended when he saw that the other man was severely wounded, so badly wounded that the German soldier was humanly touched by his condition. He gave him a drink from his canteen, and the man gave him a look of gratitude. The Englishman then indicated that he wanted him to open his breast pocket. He did so, and an envelope containing pictures of this man's family fell out. He obviously wanted to look at them once more. In that moment before the English soldier died, the German held up before him the pictures of his wife, his children, and his mother.

"In that incident," continues Barr, "there was the revelation of another dimension to the enemy. He was not only an enemy, but he was also one who was loved and loved, and lived another life as father and husband and son. The German soldier was not prompted to have mercy on his enemy as his enemy—if he kept only that in mind, he could not love him. It was not his behavior as an enemy that provoked a warm response, but rather awareness that this man was both more and less than an enemy. That encounter provided a different way of seeing him, a transformation of perspective which revealed in his enemy that dimension of his life, potential or real, which prompted love."[16]

9. *Athletic or sporting illustrations.* The modern world has often been described as being intoxicated with sports. More people watch organized athletic events each week than attend church. It makes sense, therefore, for the preacher to use occasional illustrations from the sporting world. The apostle Paul frequently referred in his letters to the athletic contests of his day—primarily races and gladiatorial combat—and those metaphors are still among the most frequently quoted passages in Paul's writings. Ministers who have been strong sports enthusiasts will have the best backlog of information and stories for this kind of illustration, but all of us have knowledge of at least some kind of sport. Tell a fishing story and a dozen persons in the congregation will comment on it afterward. Use an illustration about tennis or golfing or jogging and the feedback will be even greater. Here, as an example, is a jogging illustration:

Praying, for the Christian, is a lot like the sport of jogging. One doesn't become an expert in it overnight. At first you think, "I can never master this. Whatever possessed me to think I could?" But as the days go by and you stay with it, you find yourself gradually inching up to go the distance. It becomes easier and easier to warm up and get in the pace. Finally the time comes when you have to pray or die, just as some people have to run or die. It is an over-mastering urge. And when you are doing it — either praying or running — you enter a trancelike state that is pure bliss. Everything in you seems purified by it. You wonder, "How did I ever live before I learned to do this?" And you know you will never stop.

10. *Artistic or musical illustrations.* Just as there are many athletes or sports followers in every crowd, there are many persons who have an interest in the arts. They will respond particularly well to illustrations that involve paintings, sculpture, music, and dance. For them, the beauty of art passes almost insensibly into the province of religion. The sensitive minister can find ready illustrations in museums, concert halls, and the lives of artists and musicians. I was struck once, at a time when I was working on a sermon about the cross, by Grünewald's painting *Crucifixion*, which I saw in the National Gallery in Washington. The body of Christ appeared to have some discoloration upon it. I looked closely. Grünewald had made him a leper! There he was, on the cross, with leprosy! The people around him had infected him. What a powerful illustration, I thought, of the extent of the incarnation: he has come among us so fully that he has even taken the diseases of the flesh.

11. *Theatrical illustrations.* Drama, both on the stage and in the movies or on television, is a wealthy source of sermon illustrations. Western drama was born in the church, in the pageants presented on holy days. It is only natural, therefore, for the preacher to turn to the works of the playwright for support in preaching the gospel. It is always helpful, when a theatrical illustration is used, for people to have seen the drama referred to. But it is not necessary. Skillfully used, the apt quotation or description of a scene can impress a listener in the congregation almost as much as if he or she had witnessed a performance of the play. Once, when preach-

ing on the meaninglessness of life without Christ, I cited Eugene Ionesco's brilliant tour de force, *The Chairs*, in which an old man and woman have invited numerous unseen guests to their home atop a lighthouse in order for the old man to deliver to them the summation of his life's philosophy. The man and woman usher many important persons into the room, bringing more and more chairs in for them to occupy. Finally, when there is no more room for more chairs, the Orator arrives. Not trusting his own voice to deliver this important message, the old man has employed a professional speaker to say what he wishes to say. There is a hush as the old man announces the beginning of the speech. Then, surprisingly, the old man and woman leap from the window to their deaths below. The Orator paces back and forth, clears his throat, and faces the audience. The speaking will be even more dramatic, now that the old man has gone and entrusted everything to him. He opens his mouth. "Arr-g-hh-u-a-a-a." The Orator is a deaf-mute and cannot speak at all. It is the summation of the old man's philosophy. He was completely cynical about life. The curtains close, and the audience is left with the emptiness of modern agnosticism.

12. *Other cultural illustrations.* There are numerous other manifestations of modern culture that offer useful sermon illustrations. Advertisements, game shows, popular works of nonfiction, gossip columns, book reviews, comedy programs, and television specials are only a few. They reflect the nature of our times like bits of glass in a great mosaic, and using illustrations from them helps to capture the spirit of the environment in sermons which will both identify the limitations of the environment and help people to transcend it. Numerous sermons are improved by references to such television specials as *Roots* and *Holocaust*, which have been viewed by many persons in the average congregation. Younger ministers, I find, often use effective illustrations from contemporary music. Some are even bold enough to sing the songs. Harold Warlick, when he was pastor of Seventh and James Baptist Church in Waco, Texas, began a sermon with a reference to a country-music song called "Middle-Age Crazy" about a man

who hit middle age and suddenly broke out of all his former bonds, buying a sports car and living a wild life. It was a perfect introduction to the widespread problem in our culture of people's desperate search for life and immortality when they reach their forties.

13. *Epistolary illustrations.* Often the minister can "set off" a point in a sermon perfectly by quoting from a letter he or she has received from someone. Carlyle Marney, minister of Myers Park Baptist Church in Charlotte, North Carolina, preached a sermon on "The Recovery of Courage," which was addressed to the church and called for people to recognize again the glory and responsibility that God has entrusted to the church. In the course of talking about the church as God's channel of redemption, he said:

> Months ago John DeFoore wrote from Edinburgh to say the same thing in easier words:
>> Today I stood in Rainey Hall amidst its traditional, stately, quiet, stern beauty. I have never seen as many colors, nationalities and races, nor heard as many different tongues and dialects. No light, except a dimness that filtered through smoky stained glass windows. And then tall gray-haired Watts stood up and called all the way to heaven — as if he were Moses and all the nations waited on his prayer. He prayed for . . . *the redemption* of the whole world! Something in my soul stirred that had never moved before.
> John was just in Church, that's all. It ought to happen to you. It does happen to you when the church gets its courage back and is the Church. And this you do not have to advertise in newspapers. Not when the church is Church.[17]

14. *Personal illustrations.* These are the ones, I confess, that I like best. Stories from men's and women's experiences, from children's experiences, narrated by the persons they happened to, shared by the preacher. There is a warmth about them that makes them very appealing. They give an honest ring to the gospel that does not come from anything else. They make the gospel seem real, touchable, truly incarnate. They have the quality of *witness*, of personal presence, that cannot come from another source.

Sometimes they are from the preacher's own experience, like this example from David H. C. Read's sermon "Too Much Talk?" in which he is speaking of the effects of verbal inflation in the modern world:

> Do we talk too much? One of my first impressions when returning home after five years in a prison camp was that everyone was talking, talking, talking, about nothing in particular. We had, without realizing it, gradually eliminated all unnecessary chatter. We spoke only to communicate information, or when we deliberately wanted a discussion to pass the time. I see now that talk is a lubricant in a society where we don't know each other very well.[18]

Usually "personal illustrations" are from the experience of others, reported to the preacher. Here is one I am saving for the right sermon. It was told to me by a man I met in Pine Bluff, Arkansas. He was a gunner in the nose bubble of a B-17 plane during World War II. The pilot was landing the plane on a narrow strip in the jungle. The man in the nose bubble saw that there was a ditch across the runway. "I knew it was curtains," he said. "I tried to warn the pilot, but I couldn't speak fast enough. When I finally switched on the intercom, I knew the pilot had seen it. He was praying, 'God, don't let me panic, don't let me panic.' Somehow he managed to bounce the plane on the ground and into the air again, leaping the ditch. I have often thought of that prayer and prayed it myself in the years since. Not for anything tangible — just not to panic."

The preacher who listens carefully to the experiences of others and then uses them in sermons is like the honeybee extracting pollen from one flower and bearing it to another — he or she helps flowers to bloom across the whole field of human life and brings to fruit in our time the seeds planted by the church through the ages.

There is only one caution: don't use the stories of others indiscreetly. Never tell a story that puts someone else in a bad light or reveals a truth about a person that the person would not wish disclosed. It is a good idea, whatever the story, to ask the person or persons involved in it for permission to retell the story publicly. Most people are glad to feel that they are contributing to the sermon in this way, and asking avoids any embarrassment that might come from an unwanted revelation.

WHERE TO FIND ILLUSTRATIONS

Most preachers prepare between forty and one hundred sermons each year. Where can one possibly find enough illustrations for that many sermons? The obvious temptation to the average minister is to find them in other people's sermons and in collections of illustrations. In general it is best to beware of this temptation. One may occasionally repeat a good story or remark from another minister's sermon — no less a figure then J. Wallace Hamilton did it in nearly every sermon, giving credit where credit was due — but the long-range effect of such "borrowing" is to induce a sense of dependency and even inferiority in the preacher. It is far better to learn to find your own illustrations.

James Stewart is of the same opinion. He writes:

> The question may well be raised, How is the preacher to obtain an adequate store of illustrative material? I would warn you against being content to allow others to do this garnering for you. Ready-made collections of illustrations are a snare. Omnibus volumes of sermon anecdotes are the last refuge of a bankrupt intelligence. The best illustrations are those which come to you as the harvest of your own reading and observation.[19]

J. H. Hammerton is equally adamant. "I once inherited a book entitled *A Thousand Things to Say in Sermons*," he says. "I am glad to be able to report that I have not said one of them."[20]

The question remains: Where does one find the many illustrations that are needed? The answer is: One finds them everywhere.

1. *In reading.* At least half the illustrations most preachers use come from their reading — from books, magazines, and newspapers. Clever preachers soon learn the reading sources that provide the most illustrations and manage to spend at least part of their reading time with those sources. Through the years, for example, I have found that *Reader's Digest* and *Grit* are invaluable mines of illustrative material. One doesn't even have to have a good eye for seeing usable stories and bits of information there — they lie about like nuggets on top of the ground. And there are certain authors who, for me, are invariably rich with material: Frederick Buechner, Albert Camus, Annie Dillard, Nikos Kazantzakis,

Madeleine L'Engle, Mary Richards, and Elie Wiesel, among others. Their writings are simply studded with memorable quotations and gemlike stories. There is, in fact, almost nothing the preacher reads that may not yield an illustration, whether it is a seed catalog or a church bulletin.

2. *In listening.* Preachers are known to be talkers more than listeners. But if only we learn to listen to people, we shall find that they have many stories to tell, many important things to say, and that these become almost instant fodder for sermons. I have described the preacher as a honeybee carrying pollen from one flower to another. That is one of our primary functions in the ministry. Ours is an age of desperate loneliness, of great isolation and individualism. When we listen to this person and that one and another one, and then tell their stories in the pulpit, we are helping to eliminate the distance between them and to produce in them a sense of community. We should listen even to children and young people. Telling their stories bridges a gap between the generations. And they have so much to share with us. Their insights are often fresher and keener than our own. I shall never forget the moment when our family was standing before one of the great Spanish crucifixion scenes in the Prado. The painting, like so many Spanish works of art, was dark and brooding, unlike the sunlit plains of Spain. Christ hung on the cross. In the lower foreground a woman knelt. "Who is that?" asked our six-year-old. "That's Mary, Jesus' mother," we explained. He was quiet for a second or two. Then he said, very solemnly, "That must have hurted her." Since then I have not been able to read Simeon's words to Mary, "a sword will pierce through your own soul also" (Luke 2:35), without remembering that observation.

3. *In observing.* The word "observation" is the clue to another way the preacher finds illustrations. Interesting material for illustrations lies all around us. We miss far more of it than we see, because we have not learned to be observant. Road signs, advertisements, interesting buildings, flower arrangements, traffic patterns, ball games, nature, the behavior of insects, animals, and people—the world is simply full of phenomena that are usable when we write sermons.

121

Gerald Kennedy preached a sermon entitled "In Search of a Plot" about the apparent randomness and meaninglessness of life we experience until we find in Christ the eternal purpose of God and see the world from a new perspective. He began the sermon with an illustration that had literally come across his desk in the morning mail:

> There came to my desk, sometime ago, a literary magazine with a very curious announcement about a novel by Marc Saporta, a French experimentalist—whatever that is. The title is *Composition #1*. The book is unbound and comes in an envelope with its pages unnumbered. The reader shuffles the pages as he would a deck of cards and according to this chance arrangement, the story will take shape.[21]

It came to him, continued Kennedy, that here was a literary device reflecting the spirit of the time. People assume that life has no real meaning and that the sequence of its events is in no way ordered or significant. The sermon was on its way. It was a vivid beginning.

4. *In reflecting.* The preacher needs not only the power of observation to find illustrations but the power of reflection, of meditation on images and experiences that have been stored in the mind sometimes for years. When the preacher learns to use this power and can ransack past experiences and feelings for present sermons, his or her past becomes a golden storehouse of sermon material. William Tuck was preaching a sermon about finding the meaning of life in the risks we take for the kingdom of God. He recalled a summer afternoon with his family at an amusement park. He and his wife followed the children up the high steps to the top of a giant slide. They were tempted to turn back. Their hearts in their mouths, they let go and rode down the slide. It was an amazing experience. But they had seen other people arriving at the top of the slide turn back. These people had missed the excitement. It was a beautiful illustration about life and taking risks.[22]

Bryant Kirkland had been at Fifth Avenue Presbyterian Church in New York for more than fifteen years. But when he prepared a sermon entitled "Look Fear in the Eye," he remembered something from his previous pastorate in Tulsa, Oklahoma. He was talking about the importance of facing fears and giving them names. Then he said:

> I remember one time in the Tulsa church when I was studying late at night. I was all alone in that vast plant when I heard a sharp retort like an explosion. I said to myself what every bombardier said in World War II, "I'm going to get out of here." I got out of the building fast. The church had been robbed a few weeks before. I figured that this might be a return visit. As the door of the church closed behind me, I said, "This is no way for a Presbyterian minister to behave." Outside in the midnight air, I mused, "Your duty as a responsible officer of the church is to go back in and find out what happened." I opened the door loudly. I did not want to surprise any burglars at their work! I turned on the lights and walked from floor to floor to check each room. . . . At first I ran, as anyone else would. That was a healthy thing to do. The corrosion of anxiety would have set in if I had just gone home and said to myself, "The Lord will take care of that. There is nothing wrong. I didn't really hear anything." Actually, I went to the very top tower room and all the way down to the subbasement where the air conditioning equipment was. I could not find anybody or anything, so I went home in peace. I tell you this because it is an honest experience. I faced the fear. I gave it a name. I made an appropriate response. I got myself together and went back into the church to deal with the unknown problem which I feared.[23]

We all have enormous resources for sermon illustrations we seldom tap — in the lifetime of experiences lying behind the present moment. We simply have to learn to reflect and recall appropriate incidents that will furnish us with the material we need.

It has already been said that personal experiences are very important in the sermon, provided (*a*) they are not used too frequently, say, more than once or twice in the same sermon, and (*b*) they are not used to represent the preacher in a particularly good light. This last point is especially important. If the preacher employs illustrations that exalt the preacher, people soon get the message that the preacher has ego problems. If, on the other hand, the illustrations reveal the human side of the preacher, as in the case of Kirkland's fear, they help people to remember that the preacher is one of them, and this gives the gospel a new attractiveness for them. Brooks said that preaching is "truth through personality," not through what we *wish* our personalities were.

In short, there is simply no place where we cannot find helpful illustrations for our sermons if we but have eyes to see and ears to hear. The world is full of illustrations. We have only to see them and gather them up.

SAVING ILLUSTRATIONS

We shall say something later about saving general material for preaching, but this is the appropriate time to say a word about how the preacher can save illustrations for later use. Saving is important. Our powers of reflection and recall are limited. Old Alexander Whyte, the great Scottish preacher, when someone would ask him how he saved material, always tapped his head, indicating that he remembered it, because he did not like to fool with notebooks and filing cases. He was an acknowledged genius and used many wonderful illustrations. But one cannot help suspecting that he would have been even better and have used even more of those wonderful illustrations if he had had a workable system of storing material.

There is no single way of preserving illustrations that will suit all persons alike. Some ministers have kept what were formerly called "commonplace books"—large notebooks or scrapbooks into which they entered, sometimes by hand and sometimes in torn-out bits of pages, the ideas and illustrations that came day by day. Some have favored interleaving their Bibles — pasting blank sheets of paper among the biblical pages, on which they could then write the illustrations near to the Scripture texts they illustrated — or keeping notes in certain wide-margin Bibles published for precisely this sort of note-keeping. Others, like Ernest Campbell, have preferred carrying small pocket notebooks into which they entered material as it came to them in the course of a day, then preserving all these little notebooks in a convenient place to be consulted from time to time for a review of their contents. Still others have carried about with them pads of paper or cards on which they entered ideas and illustrations, later tearing off the used pages and dropping them into a box or entering them in some kind of filing system. And, of course, there are those orderly souls who manage to pop everything — notes, scraps of newspaper or magazine pages, photocopies of book pages — into a grand filing system labeled topically for easy location whenever the material is needed.

The important thing is for each preacher to find a system that works for him or her and then work the system. Consistency is everything. To be inconsistent is like fishing with broken nets — the best ones always get away from us.

Here is a valuable suggestion about illustrations found in books. Learn to make your own index to the books in your library. Use the flyleaf or the inside of the hard cover. Jot down brief notes about the passages you wish to recall or to be able to locate in the future, giving the page numbers clearly. Then, when you are writing a sermon and think, "Ah, I remember that so-and-so had a lovely illustration of this in her book," you can go to the shelf, take down the book, and quickly recover the exact wording of the material. I have followed this practice for years and find it immensely helpful. Sometimes I take down half a dozen books before beginning a sermon and refresh myself on the contents. This not only provides material I need at the moment, it imprints more indelibly on my mind the existence of material for future occasions.

HOW MANY ILLUSTRATIONS
TO USE

Suppose the preacher has a keen eye and ear, coupled with a strong system of preserving and recalling material. Won't that lead to the temptation to use too much illustrative material in the sermon? Yes, it sometimes does. There are sermons that appear to be like pearl necklaces — a string of jewels with only a slight knot in each end to hold them together. Even a master preacher like Harry Emerson Fosdick often used too many illustrations, especially later in his career when he had managed to accumulate a great deal of material. Illustrations have a way of *accreting* to a sermon — of building up through successive uses of the same sermon. When Fosdick again preached the same sermon he had preached years earlier, it invariably had more illustrations added to the original ones.

Today, when the fifteen- or twenty-minute sermon is more the rule than the exception, it is best to restrict oneself to using a single illustration for each point of the sermon. If there are two points, two illustrations; three points, three illustrations. This is not a hard-and-fast rule, of course. If one has two brief illustrations, they may be used in place of one longer one. The preacher simply has to use his or her own sense about such matters. But it is a good idea to look hard at one's illustrations, especially in the latter years, when one's store is larger than it was in the beginning.

Henry Sloane Coffin said that one reason for writing out his sermons was to be able to take an exacting look at his illustrations:

> In writing I find also that a number of my aforeprepared illustrations can profitably be discarded. One wants no more than are necessary to illumine one's thought. Corinna is said to have counseled the poet Pindar "to sow with the hand, not with the full sack."[24]

Some sermons, because of their subject matter, are more illustrative by nature than others. A sermon on Jonah or Hosea, for example, is obviously rather pictorial to begin with and will need less illustrative material to make it clear and memorable. The same is true of sermons based on the parables of Jesus. They *are* illustrations and require little support from other illustrations. A sermon from Deuteronomy or Isaiah or the Sermon on the Mount, on the other hand, will generally need illumination from other sources.

MISCELLANEOUS SUGGESTIONS

Illustrations are among the most personal parts of a sermon. They reflect the insight, taste, and convictions of the minister in a way that few can miss. Therefore it is impossible to issue inflexible rules about the choice and use of illustrative material. It may be helpful, however, to provide some general suggestions that the individual preacher can ponder and apply to his or her preaching as they seem to merit application.

1. *Choose the illustration that is right on target, not the one that merely approximates it.* It was once said, at a time when American

golfers were regularly beating British golfers, that the British golfers shot for the green while the Americans shot for the pin. Shoot for the pin with your illustrations. If they merely land on the edge of the green, reject them. An illustration that does not go to the center of a point interferes with the lines of force in a sermon; it hinders the thought and disrupts the natural progress.

2. *Never use an illustration merely because it is a compelling anecdote.* Preachers have been known to go in search of a sermon text and outline because they had an overpowering story to use. This is a poor approach to the preaching task. In the long run it corrupts the vision of the preacher, so that the preacher no longer listens for a word from God but yields to every attractive illustration that comes down the road.

3. *Avoid illustrations that swallow the sermon.* Some illustrations are so long and powerful that they literally overwhelm the remainder of the sermon. It is better, if the preacher cannot resist using such an illustration, to let it *be* the sermon on a particular Sunday instead of allowing it to destroy the thrust of another sermon by coupling the two together.

4. *Reflect on your illustrations to make certain they do not raise issues you may not wish to raise.* Sometimes there are secondary elements in an illustration that capture more attention from listeners than the primary elements. Henry Ward Beecher was aware of this phenomenon and used it for his own purposes; he often employed illustrations with antislavery propaganda in them, and then, if questioned, feigned not to have realized what he was doing. The preacher who is not conscious of this potentiality in illustrations, however, may find that a particular illustration, instead of helping people to concentrate on the subject at hand, has started them off in another direction altogether.

5. *Do not use illustrations that have to be explained.* I have heard preachers consume more time explaining an illustration than the time required to present the illustration itself. This is like having to turn on a light to see the light one has already turned on. There should be such clarity in an illustration that it does its work without comment — or at least with no more than a passing remark.

6. *Do not press illustrations for extra mileage.* That is, do not attempt to extract extra duty from them or expect them to answer for more meaning than is on ·heir surface. As Charles Spurgeon said, "If an illustration will go with you a mile, do not compel it to go with you twain." A perfectly good illustration can be ruined in its effect by a preacher who is bent on squeezing more than its obvious meaning from it. As it was said of some unbearably tedious medieval preacher, he could not resist "allegorizing the allegorization."

7. *Employ illustrations with sentiment, but reject those that are full of sentimentality.* Admittedly there is a fine line between sentiment and sentimentality, but the preacher must attempt to draw it. Pathos is a useful and dignified part of Christian preaching; bathos is not. The tear that comes to the eye in a sermon should come because deep reservoirs of feeling and belief have been tapped, not because someone has held a vial of ammonia under our noses. Illustrations, as we have said, often carry the emotional strength of a sermon. They are easily subject to abuse if the preacher is seeking to manipulate the congregation according to his or her own will for their behavior. What the preacher should legitimately try to do is to put people in touch with their own best instincts and higher judgment. Let the illustrations aim at that, not at producing a maudlin situation in which their wills are at the mercy of the preacher's.

8. *With the last caveat in mind, arrange the illustrative material in the sermon so that the emotional level is ascending, not descending.* That is, it is not wise to use an illustration in point one that has an emotional intensity of ten, then use one in point three that has an intensity of only seven. The emotional involvement of the sermon should grow steadily stronger as the sermon progresses. Therefore it is a good idea to avoid using powerful illustrations early in the sermon or weak ones late in the sermon.

9. *Suit your illustrations to the place and audience.* As Ian Macpherson has pointed out, some church buildings seem almost intended to frustrate the use of stories:

> There are ecclesiastical edifices in which it would be well-nigh impossible to employ a kindling illustration — gloomy, sepulchral,

half-lit, draughty caves, in which the only sort of ministry consonant with the surroundings would be a raven-like croaking about
human mortality! Happily, there are other sanctuaries which are
highly conducive to a pictorial mode of preaching and in which it
is a pleasure to illuminate one's message with living word-pictures.[25]

Similarly there are congregations whose sense of reserve and
sophistication is such that they do not respond easily to the same
illustrations that would work marvelously well in a rural parish.
The preacher must simply be a sensible person about this and
adapt his or her illustrations to the taste and manners of the
setting.

10. *Never employ illustrations that show other persons in a bad
light.* Nothing will turn people off faster than an anecdote or a
remark that may be interpreted as a slur upon a person or persons
of another race, nationality, or religion. Many a careless preacher
has alienated someone in the congregation by a thoughtless allusion to another denomination or faith. It is even possible to hurt
people's feelings by alluding unsympathetically to a particular
profession, university, or way of life. One minister I know used an
illustration that put cats in a dubious light and was redressed by
three cat owners as they left the church that day. It is impossible
to avoid all misunderstandings in what we say, but we should at
least weigh our illustrations for potential offenses.

11. *Do not use illustrations involving persons in your congregation unless you have their permission.* Nothing will destroy a
minister's counseling relationships faster than the feeling that he
or she does not honor the strictest confidentiality about pastoral
matters. It is a good idea, even when someone has given permission for using a remark or a story, to indicate to the congregation
that permission has been granted. That way other persons will not
worry about a breach of confidence. Some ministers make it a rule
never to use a personal illustration from a present parish until at
least five years have elapsed, and others make it a rule not to use
one in the same parish at all. With the high rate of mobility in
today's culture, one hardly feels safe in using a personal illustration
even after moving to another city. A minister of my acquaintance
moved to another church more than a thousand miles from the one

he had served and felt perfectly safe in using confidential stories from his former parish. One Sunday, after a particularly revealing reference to a counselee in the old church, someone said to him, "That was so-and-so you were talking about, wasn't it? I once lived in that community."

12. *Never use untrue illustrations unless you introduce them by saying, "Let's suppose . . ." or "Can't we imagine . . ."* It is tempting, if a minister has a good imagination, to construct a story and pass it off as true in a sermon. There is nothing wrong with fabricating stories — the parables of Jesus, as far as we know, were all imagined. But it is wrong for the minister to pretend that things are true when they aren't, and doing so inevitably erodes the minister's own sense of truth and honesty.

13. *Do not employ trite or hackneyed illustrations.* Overused illustrations, silly illustrations, and incredible illustrations are an offense in any sermon. They cheapen the message. They also consume time that might be given to better illustrations. "A sermon without illustrations is like a house without windows," said Buttrick. "A sermon with trivial or bathetic illustrations is worse: it is like a house with the windows broken, and the holes stuffed with rags and straw."[26] This is one very good reason for not using "omnibus volumes of sermon anecdotes." Most of these are full of silly stuff, and the better stories in them have been told so often that there are always people in the congregation who have heard them before.

14. *Don't use other preachers' illustrations without giving credit for them.* This is a matter of both honesty and civility. I have heard ministers employing other ministers' stories, ones I had heard from their original sources, as if they were their own, even to the point of having happened to them. It is pathetic when ministers are so desperate for approval that they will poach upon others' material and adopt it under their own names. There is no need for this. It takes nothing from the sermon to preface an illustration by saying, "Someone has said . . ." or, "A colleague has told this story . . ." And the preservation of one's integrity is an important issue. It affects one's feelings about oneself and helps to keep a necessary sense of order in one's private universe.

15. *Do work at the transitions that lead into your illustrations.* There is a knack to getting into the illustration. If you rush in too boldly without preparation, some people in the congregation will miss the connection between the abstract point and the remark or story. If you prepare too elaborately for the entrance, some will find your introduction tedious and your illustration anticlimactic. Here again is an advantage of writing the sermon: You can study your transitions to be certain they are smooth, varied, and effective.

In summary, illustrations are a very important part of the minister's craft of preaching. They abound everywhere, like manna from heaven, for the preacher with eyes to see and ears to hear. Used properly, they will illuminate any sermon, no matter how profound or serious, so that even a childlike mind can follow it. They will impart a sense of reality to the sermon that it might otherwise lack. They will help people see how the theology of the sermon can function in their own lives. The minister ignores them at his or her own peril. I have never heard a good sermon illustrator who was not at least a passable preacher. And I have never heard anyone who was not able to use illustrations — including some renowned theologians and biblical scholars — to whom even a generous listener could give passing marks.

NOTES

1. Robert J. Smithson, ed., *My Way of Preaching* (London: Pickering and Inglis, n.d.), p. 15.

2. In Ian Macpherson, *The Art of Illustrating Sermons* (Nashville: Abingdon Press, 1964), p. 13.

3. Smithson, ed., *My Way of Preaching*, p. 67.

4. Macpherson, *The Art of Illustrating Sermons*, p. 15.

5. In G. Paul Butler, ed., *Best Sermons, 1947–1948* (New York: Harper & Brothers, 1947), pp. 95–96.

6. William Barclay, *William Barclay: A Spiritual Autobiography* (Grand Rapids: Wm. B. Eerdmans Publishing Co., 1975), p. 16.

7. Ibid., p. 65.

8. Ibid., p. 6.

9. *The Churchman*, August–September, 1979, p. 7.

10. Bryant Kirkland, "Look Fear in the Eye," published sermon, Fifth Avenue Presbyterian Church, New York City, n.d.

11. In G. Paul Butler, ed., *Best Sermons, 1962* (Princeton: D. Van Nostrand Co., 1962), p. 24.

12. François Mauriac, *What I Believe*, tr. Wallace Fowlie (New York: Farrar, Strauss & Co., 1963), p. 39.

13. Martin Buber, *I and Thou*, tr. R. G. Smith (New York: Charles Scribner's Sons, 1958), p. 95.

14. George Bernanos, *The Diary of a Country Priest*, tr. Pamela Morris (New York: Doubleday & Co., Image Books, 1954), p. 41.

15. Dostoevsky's epitaph for his mother's tomb, cited in C. M. Woodhouse, *Dostoievsky* (New York: Roy Publishers, 1951), p. 75.

16. Browne Barr, *East Bay and Eden: Contemporary Sermons* (Nashville: Abingdon Press, 1963), pp. 139–140.

17. In G. Paul Butler, ed., *Best Sermons, Volume IX* (Princeton: D. Van Nostrand Co., 1964), pp. 70–71.

18. David H. C. Read, *Religion Without Wrappings* (Grand Rapids: Wm. B. Eerdmans Publishing Co., 1970), p. 34.

19. James S. Stewart, *Heralds of God: A Practical Book on Preaching* (New York: Charles Scribner's Sons, 1956), p. 144.

20. In Macpherson, *The Art of Illustrating Sermons*, p. 79.

21. In Butler, *Best Sermons, Volume IX*, p. 62.

22. William P. Tuck, *The Struggle for Meaning* (Valley Forge, Pa.: Judson Press, 1977), p. 136.

23. Kirkland, "Look Fear in the Eye," pp. 2–3.

24. In Donald Macleod, *Here Is My Method: The Art of Sermon Construction* (Westwood, N.J.: Fleming H. Revell Co., 1952), p. 55.

25. Macpherson, *The Art of Illustrating Sermons*, p. 185.

26. George A. Buttrick, *Jesus Came Preaching* (New York: Charles Scribner's Sons, 1931), p. 159.

7

Matters of Style and Delivery

Style is the preacher's signature on the sermon. It is the combination of rhythm, metaphor, diction, voice, and pauses that puts such an individual stamp on the sermon that those familiar with the preacher would know whose it was even if they were blindfolded. It is like style in anything else — it expresses the personality of its author so completely that anyone else found using it would be immediately dubbed an imitator or a thief. Anyone who is great in any field of endeavor has a recognizable style — Hemingway in the novel, Rodin in sculpture, Bernstein in music, DiMaggio in baseball, Picasso in painting. Part of their greatness lies in the purity of the equation between their lives and their art. Their art is what it is because they are who they are; it expresses their individuality. The same is true of the art of great preachers. It is so accurate an extension of them that it captures and reveals their personalities. Think of the outstanding preachers of the nineteenth century — Beecher, Spurgeon, Brooks, Robertson — and the outstanding preachers of our own time — Whyte, Gossip, Stewart, Weatherhead, Fosdick, Buttrick, Scherer. Each was so distinctive that a single paragraph from a sermon would have been clue enough to identify the sermon as his. Indeed, their styles were so well known that many lesser ministers, stuck in their writing of a sermon, would think, "How would Brooks or Buttrick have handled this?" and then be quickly off with their preparation, prompted by a recognition of what needed to be done.

Leslie Fiedler, the critic, once said that Hemingway and

Faulkner, the two greatest novelists of America in the twentieth century, became famous by writing parodies of themselves and then ended by writing parodies of the parodies. That is an exaggerated way of saying that they found their techniques and stayed with them, honing and varying them but slightly in novel after novel. This is also what the preacher does. It is not a matter of copying the self, as Fiedler implied, or trying to repeat former successes. It is instead a sign of maturity in one's discipline, an indication that one has discovered certain things that work and is willing to use them again in the service of the art. It is foolish for any artist to remain an experimentalist throughout life, casting each work in a different style from all the others. The artist can—and *should*—continue to experiment with the range and scope of material. But constantly experimenting with technique, once one has found the tools that work, is an irresponsible use of time. That can be left to younger artists still trying to find their styles. Maturer artists have other problems to address.

The sooner preachers discover their individual styles, the sooner they are able to move into their most productive and useful years of preaching. Once they know how they work best and what their voices sound like, they become like machines that have finally warmed up and stopped vibrating so wildly; they can settle down to the task before them. Then they lose much less effort in thinking *how* they shall preach and can apply their energies to thinking *what* they will preach.

FINDING ONE'S OWN STYLE

Is discovering one's own style in preaching accidental or is it something one can work at? There is no doubt that accident plays a significant part in most of our ministries. We noted earlier that John Claypool virtually awoke one day to find himself preaching in a "confessional" style because of the illness and death of his ten-year-old daughter. Claypool says he stumbled onto a preaching method he could never forget, one in which he shared his own often blind and difficult pilgrimage with the people. Confessionalism has become part of his style. But, yes, style is also something one can work at. There are ways of discovering what works best for one, of consciously developing effective techniques, of learning to project one's own inner being into the words and phrases and images of a sermon. What some preachers discover accidentally others can discover intentionally. Only two things are required for the discovery: effort and reflection. Any preacher who is willing to apply himself or herself in these two ways can reach a new level of self-consciousness about style and will find preaching at the new level much easier and more exciting than it was before.

Here are the simple steps to be followed:

1. *You must begin by doing sustained disciplinary work on your sermons — that is, by writing them in full for a period of one year or more.* It is much easier to observe matters of style in a manuscript or typescript than on a tape recording or in one's memory. There are doubtless a few natural geniuses who can come to a great personal style for preaching without ever writing their sermons, but for most of us there is no way around the sheer labor of writing. It is in the endless struggle to think deeply and write clearly that we first begin to discover what we have to say and how we can best say it. Eventually, as you apply yourself in this manner, you get the kinks out of your system. What you produce becomes more and more your own.

It is like playing baseball. The first few times you are up at bat, the newness of the game makes you awkward and ill-disposed. Your swing is ungainly and ineffective. A great deal of effort is wasted in prodigious attempts to hit the ball well. Eventually, though, if you have any aptitude at all, you learn to time yourself better and to connect easily with the ball. Your effort is *controlled*, and the effect is much more pleasing, both to you and to your teammates.

Your first efforts at writing sermons will be disappointing to you. You will feel that you are expending more energy than you have to give to weekly sermon composition. The temptation will be to flee to some other area of parish work that is more immediately pleasurable and rewarding. But have patience. The writing will come easier. And as it does, you will begin to see certain pat-

terns in the way you work. Natural techniques will repeat themselves. You will soon learn to rely on these techniques, sharpening
them as you do. You will know how dependable they are and feel
more comfortable about preaching.

2. *Take the patterns seriously.* Pursue these emergent techniques
with the conscious intention of improving them. Apply them
thoughtfully in sermon after sermon. Vary them from time to time
in order to get a more proper estimate of their worth and power.
You may even wish to exaggerate them, and use them occasionally
in caricature form, in order to understand them better. Writers
and artists often do this, especially during their apprentice
periods. It helps them to see a technique more clearly. For example, you may have discovered that you have a penchant for describing biblical characters and situations in modern dress, somewhat
in the vein of Frederick Buechner or Clovis Chappell. Write whole
sermons in which this is the primary technique you employ; make
the situations *very* modern; take your descriptions to the extreme.
You may feel afterward that these particular sermons were unsuccessful and that you do not wish to do that again. No matter! You
are learning more about your technique. You can sacrifice a few
sermons to that. Indeed, it is the only way ever to learn anything.
We must crawl before we can walk, and walk before we can run.
It is in discovering the limits to which you can carry your style and
technique that you really understand your style and come to a
mastery of it.

3. *Once you have begun to feel comfortable with a style, abandon it occasionally to develop an alternate style.* Consciously select
some other technique you have noticed budding in the corner of
a sermon you have preached and plant it squarely in the center of
a sermon all its own. Give it a chance to grow and blossom as your
other style did. This not only provides variety in your preaching,
it helps to test your satisfaction with the style you have already
developed. In almost every art, people go through stages or periods
when new styles appear in their work. A painter may move from
expressionism to representation to a new form combining the two
previous forms. It is a matter of stages of life and work. In many

cases, evolution is an essential ingredient of growth. The preacher is not static; his or her life is constantly changing and passing through new seasons of insight and understanding. Sermon styles may need to reflect these various seasons. There will probably be a continuity of style in most preachers' sermons, once a basic style has been reached, but occasional variations in the pattern will give added strength and maturity to that particular style.

Preachers who have difficulty discerning any style or pattern in their preaching may wish to put themselves to school temporarily with some great stylists in order to become more sensitive to matters of style and technique. Benjamin Franklin, who was one of the finest prose writers in our history, learned to write by copying the *Spectator* papers of Addison and Steele. First he copied an essay. Then he laid aside both the essay and his copy and attempted to reconstruct the essay from memory. Finally he compared his reconstruction with the original, noting the deficiencies in his own effort. After a few months of this, he was able to abandon his models and write well in his own way, gradually moving away from the style of his mentors and finding one that was more suited to his native intelligence. A preacher wishing to learn by the same method might well imitate such stylists as Fosdick or Buttrick or William Sloane Coffin. I have often recommended, when a student was having trouble with a colorless personal style, that he or she study the sermons of J. Wallace Hamilton, who had an apt way with illustrative material and the interesting, lively phrase. Women preachers are at a disadvantage here, for there have been no great, widely known females in the preaching tradition to serve as models for their styles, and it is not always profitable for them to study the models offered by males. At the present time, they will be well advised to find individual sermons preached by women whose styles they find interesting and compatible and learn to imitate those. Some names of women whose work bears watching, I believe, are Ann Denham, Sue Anne Steffey Morrow, Carolyn Pitts, Glenda Webb, and Lula Creed. In the end, of course, one should give up dependence on the work of another and pursue one's own style. But sometimes beginning with the sermons of another helps one to identify the meaning of style and to begin to pursue it as an individual matter.

IMPORTANT ELEMENTS IN A PREACHING STYLE

Because it is finally an oral act whose success depends on the response of many people, preaching has certain pressures upon it that do not bear so heavily on other art forms. It must appeal to people; it must have relevance to life; and it must communicate so well that people understand its message when they hear it. In other words, one's preaching style is dictated not only by one's personality but by the congregation as well. This can make a considerable difference in the style one chooses to follow. The preacher who addresses a small, mainly rural audience will necessarily speak differently from the preacher in an urban church of several hundred members. The preacher who speaks in a cathedral will naturally develop a style different from that of the preacher in a more casual setting.

When I was a young preacher pastoring a small rural church near Renfro Valley, Kentucky, a college friend wrote to say he was coming through the area and would like to preach for a week in my church. I arranged for him to live in the home of a deacon of the church and announced the meetings. I looked forward to hearing my friend, for he had shown the promise of being a very good preacher. It turned out to be one of the most disastrous experiences I have ever had. My friend's preaching was totally different from the way I had remembered it. He carried a full manuscript into the pulpit. His eyes were on it constantly, and he waved his arms wildly and irrationally, often above the level of his head, for he was straining to see the manuscript. His voice rose and fell without discernible patterns of logic or emphasis. The entire performance was so frightening that many children in the congregation refused to come back after the first service. It was a miserable week. Attendance waned dreadfully. Only my friend remained cheerful through it all, content to be preaching and gaining experience.

I could not imagine what had happened to transform him from the modest, reasonable young preacher I had known into this unintelligible ranter who was holding forth in our church each night. At last, on the final evening, I discovered what had happened. My friend and I were left alone in a farmhouse while our hosts went out to feed and milk their cattle. My friend retired to a bedroom to practice his sermon. In idle search of something to read, I reached into his briefcase and took out a book. It was a collection of sermons by Carlyle Marney. I began to read. Lo and behold, there was Monday night's sermon! Further: there was Wednesday night's sermon! Again: Sunday morning's sermon! Every sermon we had heard was there. Not trusting his own mettle, my friend had apparently decided to preach Marney's sermons instead. It was a dismal mistake. Marney had given the sermons in a large city church before a congregation that included many college and seminary professors. Even there, I think he had shown off a bit, using a more extravagant diction than was necessary. And my friend, poor well-meaning fellow, had presumed to deliver the same sermons to an audience of farm folk, most of whom had not even graduated from high school. What is more, he had tried to do it with his head buried in a manuscript and his arms flailing the air as if he were a man drowning!

Preaching is not something one does alone. The audience too is involved in it. The audience has one end of the rope and we have the other. If we tug on the rope and do not feel a responsive pull from the other end, something is wrong.

My friend's sad experience does not disprove the worth of a manuscript. It only proves he had the wrong kind of manuscript and didn't know how to use a manuscript when he had it. If it had been *his* manuscript and he had used it properly—in this case, by leaving it behind in his room and not taking it into a rural pulpit—he would have learned an important lesson: that he needed to speak in simpler, more understandable terms to those gentle people from the country. Feeling no response from the other end of the rope, he would have adjusted his style, and everything would have come up roses in the end.

Audiences vary widely. Are there any rules for developing a good style that will be suitable among all of them? The answer is yes. There are certain traits of a good style that we should aim at in the preparation of every sermon we intend to preach. They apply whether we shall be speaking before a crossroads audience in Lenox, Iowa, or a university audience in New York City.

1. *Write your manuscript in an oral style, not a written style.* The sermon will be spoken, not read. Or at least it will be spoken before it is read by anyone in the congregation. Therefore it should read like a spoken sermon, not an essay or a dissertation. This means there may be broken phrases, sentences ending in prepositions, rhetorical questions, and colloquial usages — all hallmarks of extemporaneous speech. It does not mean *careless* prose — only *casual* prose. There is a difference. Someone has said, "When we preach we use a conversational style. Yet it is not just any conversation, it is *edited* conversation, *high* conversation." The preacher does not simply throw it together, as though the words did not matter. On the contrary, the preacher works very hard at this conversational style. Felix Frankfurter, one of the great justices of the United States Supreme Court, was noted as a brilliant conversationalist. Once he kept a taxi driver waiting outside a party for thirty minutes after they arrived. Someone noticed Frankfurter sitting in the cab and came out to bring him in. "Not yet," he said, "I have not completed my extemporaneous remarks." That is the idea — conversation well prepared!

Henry Sloane Coffin, who was invariably a manuscript preacher, "talked" his sentences aloud as he prepared them, in order to keep the style conversational. Hartley Hall, president of Union Theological Seminary in Richmond, did the same thing when he was minister of Westminster Presbyterian Church in Nashville. "I know people who hear me in the office think I'm crazy," he said, "but I now spend more time talking through my sermons and rewriting them in conversational style than I spend getting the ideas and writing them down the first time."

There are two principal advantages to writing the sermon in an oral style. One is that people *hear* an oral style better than a written one and experience a freshness in it that is missing from the written style. The other is that the preacher finds an oral manuscript easier to preach than a manuscript in the written style. The words come off the page more easily and leap out to do their work in the congregation. A sermon written like an essay sounds like an essay when it is delivered, regardless of how skillful the preacher is.

2. *Aim at simplicity of speech.* This may appear to be redundant advice, for an oral style is generally simpler than a written one. But some preachers could improve even their oral performances by achieving greater simplicity. There is something about the ministry — about being called on to speak in public a great deal — that causes many preachers to become false and rhetorical in their diction. They lose the sense of simplicity and directness that comes from being silent, from taking time to ponder the great mysteries of life. "How many idle words there are in the average sermon," said Buttrick, "— words that do no work, that are not felt, that are merely sound."[1]

Read Hemingway's *The Old Man and the Sea*, noting the language. There are probably fewer than a hundred trisyllabic words in the entire masterpiece. Most of the words are three-, four-, and five-letter words derived from hard, clear Anglo-Saxon forebears. They do their work solidly, quietly, unobtrusively. Behind them, one can smell the salt air, hear the rhythm of the sea, feel the depth and mystery of the water. They do not interfere with the meaning. They say what the author wishes to say and bow aside, like good and obedient servants. The reader is left alone with the thought, a picture, a feeling, an impact.

That is the way it ought to be with preaching. We should never parade our finest language for people, as though it were marshaled out for a showing, but hide it behind the rough and serviceable words that become transparent to thought the instant they are spoken. Suppose Jesus had said, "A particular member of the august race *Homo sapiens* happened to have in his possession two offspring, in favor not unlike himself" instead of, "A certain man had two sons." What chance would there have been for the survival of the parable? We are not in the ministry to display pedantry but to preach the gospel, and when words get in our way, the gospel is liable to be taken away from us and put in the mouths of babes and sucklings.

"I counsel you," said Herbert Farmer to his audience at the Warrack Lectures, "go through your sermon when it is written and look hard and long at every abstract word. Often it will not be possible to alter it to a concrete word, for abstract terms are part of the indispensable coinage of thought and even the simplest mind uses them; but it may be possible to alter it to one more familiar. Yet even so, it is surprising how often an abstract term can be altered to a concrete, and how great is the resultant gain in vividness and power."[2]

Georges Simenon, the famous writer of detective novels, is even more ruthless with himself. For a long time his work did not sell because it was too literary. When he learned that this was his problem, he began paring all the adjectives, adverbs, and other words that were there only to make an effect. Soon his books began to sell in unprecedented number, because people could understand them. Now he says he keeps a watchful eye on all his words. If he spots a beautiful sentence, he cuts it out immediately. Its very beauty makes it suspect.[3]

Can we be less objective about our sermons? We are not in the ministry to compose memorable homilies for the ages. We are here to speak to the sick and dying, to bind up the wounded and send them back into the streets and homes of our communities, to bring the spirit of love into a world torn by hate and dissension. We shall not serve God by trying to carve elaborately beautiful sentences, but by speaking words of life and courage.

Henry Ward Beecher understood. "I have known a great many most admirable preachers," he said, "who lost almost all real sympathetic hold upon their congregations because they were too literary, too periphrastic, and too scholastic in their diction. They always preferred to use large language, rather than good Saxon English. But let me tell you, there is a subtle charm in the use of plain language that pleases people, they scarcely know why. It gives bell-notes which ring out suggestions to the popular heart. There are words that men have heard when boys at home, around the hearth and the table, words that are full of father and of mother, and full of common and domestic life. Those are the words that . . . will produce a strong influence on your auditors, giving an element of success; words which will have an effect that your hearers themselves cannot understand. For, after all, simple language is loaded down and stained through with the best testimonies and memories of life."[4]

There is the sum of it: our styles should be simple but profound, touching the deepest notes of the human heart. We should disdain affectation, always preferring the direct sentence, the unadorned verb and noun, the solid, gripping thought. Like the parables of Jesus, our speech should do its work without calling attention to itself and leave the hearer not with an impression of our fine diction but with an unforgettable word from God. When there is any question, cut. Do not be afraid of losing an important thought. If it is any good, it will come back, the next time in purer, simpler language.

3. *Strive for absolute clarity of thought.* The preacher deals with some of the subjects hardest in the world to talk about: God, love, righteousness, faith, eternity. It is no wonder that many of us often lapse into obscurity, as if it were our duty to make the mystery in our messages more mysterious still. Our own minds unclear about the subjects with which we have to deal, we simply turn the fans on our own haziness and blow it out into the congregations. "London is just now buried under a dense fog," wrote Canon Liddon to a friend. "This is commonly attributed to Dr. Westcott having opened his study-window at Westminster."[5]

There is no evidence anywhere of anybody's having ever been converted by a lack of clarity. People simply are not moved by what they cannot understand. Therefore it is essential for preachers to work at their sermons until the obscurities have been squeezed out and sound, reliable passages set in their places. A religious "noise" from the pulpit, consisting of pious-sounding phrases pronounced unctuously in a pseudo-passionate rhythm, may momentarily transport people in the way certain music does, but it does not leave them anything to feed upon when the noise stops. There is no substitute in Christian preaching for clear thinking clothed in simple language.

Young preachers are often unclear because they attempt to deal with great living themes before they have had time to think their way through the complexities of the themes. They feel compelled to address the subjects, yet have no mastery of them. They may begin existentially enough, with some illustration from their own lives or the lives of their parishioners, but soon they reach out for support to the books of illustrious theologians they have studied, and their poor people, who had tucked their napkins under their chins for a "down-home" meal of solid victuals, find themselves sputtering and choking on such indigestibles as Tillich's "ultimate concern" and Bultmann's "demythologization."

Never do that to your people. Observe a moratorium on all exegetical and theological ideas you have not had time to digest. Once they have gone through your digestive system and become an integral part of your thinking, it is all right to attempt to preach them. Until then, sit on them, no matter how much they intrigue or excite you. They will keep, if they are worth repeating, and will be all the richer for having had time to work into the fabric of your thought.

This does not mean that you should avoid tackling big themes until you are older and wiser. Big themes ought to be the constant diet of our people. But it does mean approaching the themes sensibly and dealing with them in terms of your own experience. Take the subject of death, for example. Young preachers cannot come at that topic with the self-assurance and understanding of older pastors who have lived with death day in and day out for years—and shouldn't try. But they can come at it confessionally, admitting their fear of it and their need of support from older members of the congregation. They can treat it impressionistically, though not comprehensively, describing it from their limited, personal points of view. They have, as their elders have not, lived with it all their lives on television; there was not a time when they did not see it portrayed in hospital dramas, gangster movies, and war films. They have, as their elders have not, lived under the threat of nuclear holocaust since they were infants. Therefore they have something to say on the subject of death. The important thing is that they not try to say what the elders might say, but say what they know and feel on their own.

One of the best ways to avoid obscurity in style is to be as concrete and particular as possible at all times. Don't indulge in flights of rhetoric that carry no payload. When you talk about love, talk about *particular* love. When you talk about fear, talk about *particular* fear. When you talk about the grace of God, talk about the *particular* ways in which God is graceful. Herbert Farmer once said that preaching fails when it is too small to be true, too confident to be true, and too easy to be true. Colin Morris, remembering these admonitions, adds a fourth — preaching fails when it is "too generalized to be true." "The Gospel does not cover the universal human condition, which is sordid, messy and dishevelled," he says, "with a pink mist of spirituality. Instead, it acts upon the pressure-points of individual lives, challenging attitudes to matters so down to earth as sex, ambition, power, race and money."[6] Deal with these subjects realistically and your meaning will be clear enough to people. Clear enough, if you are not pastoral in your attitude, to make them complain.

Finally, in the attempt to speak clearly in every sermon, cast an especially wary eye on the most familiar religious and theological words in your vocabulary. We are not any freer, in the ministry, from professional jargon than our colleagues in medicine and law and government. Reuel Howe and his associates at the Institute for Advanced Pastoral Studies, in Bloomfield Hills, Michigan, interviewed thousands of laypersons about what is wrong with the preaching they hear. Over and over, the laypersons responded that preachers are vague and hard to understand. Asked what they find difficult to understand, many replied that it is the arcane language — words such as "salvation," "judgment," "gospel," and "redemption."[7] We use these words so regularly that we forget how obscure they can be. Often they become mere ciphers in our own minds, casting a cloak of respectability over the barrenness of our thought processes and preventing our moving in closer to grapple more precisely with ideas. It is difficult not to use them — they are part of the vocabulary of Zion. But we can at least attempt to unpack them whenever we use them, interpreting them with current language so that everyone understands what we mean.

"I say what I mean and I mean what I say," declares Hortense the Elephant, a Dr. Seuss character. It is a good motto for a preacher: "I say what I mean and I mean what I say."

4. *Try to be interesting.* Surely one of the worst sins of the pulpit

is dullness. "What a reflection on us bunglers it is," said A. J. Gossip, "that we have so mishandled the chivalry and glory of that exciting, valorous, thrilling tale of Jesus Christ, that people are so thoroughly bored by such a very dull and stale affair as we have made of it that twenty minutes' talk about it is fully as much as they can stand, and anything more really an infliction through which they can only yawn and fidget miserably — the very people who will spend hours upon hours at a more or less silly opera, or over some transient tale! With such a subject we ought to have swept the world."[8]

The way a sermon is delivered surely has something to do with its interest level, but the way it is written also has a lot to do with its vivacity and attractiveness. Even great actors have difficulty with poor scripts. Ask yourself, as you write the sermon: "Is this living material? How can I make it more interesting than it is? What can I do to kindle in others the interest I feel?"

It is a basic flaw in most sermons that their underlying structure is not interesting — that the very way the sermons are developed is dull and tedious. They progress along such obvious lines that anyone could guess where they will go next. There is no element of surprise or suspense in them. The best-loved preachers have always followed one of two strategies: either they have had unanticipated "wrinkles" in the development of their sermons (Buttrick was a master at this) or they have used such unique ways of expressing and developing the more or less obvious points of their sermons that people listened eagerly, convinced they were hearing "what oft was thought, but ne'er so well expressed."

Novelists and playwrights, if asked about maintaining an audience's interest, would say that the task is best answered by introducing *conflict* into their work. There is a natural drama about any subject when there are opposing forces at work in it. Perhaps this is why fundamentalist preaching often seems interesting when liberal preaching does not: it keeps alive the notion of a dualism in the universe, of an eternal conflict between God and the devil, with human beings' lives hanging in the balance. Without that dualism, preaching collapses into moralism. Evil becomes bad judgment and human error. There is no longer any sense of spiritual terror and damnation. The minister becomes a therapist instead of a preacher.

This is not to suggest that liberal preachers ought to inject old revivalist language into their modern sermons. That kind of conflict would be as obvious as the conflict in a grade-C Western. It is to suggest that we might all be better preachers if we thought more deeply about the origins of good and evil in the world and saw the implications of religious commitment or lack of it in those terms. The New Testament writings are couched in dualistic language. Their vision would have been impossible apart from the drama of conflict, apocalypse, and eschatology. If we are steeped in biblical thought, our own thinking cannot help being tinged by a sense of last things.

Contemporary preachers have made one important discovery about maintaining interest in a sermon. They have learned that people are interested in sermons that deal with their felt needs and problems. "We are interested in that which involves us," said Gene Bartlett. "Let it become clear that a sermon is dealing with the living options which confront a person, and inevitably he becomes interested in the outcome."[9] Life situation preaching, focused on the hurts and aspirations of average people, has become the conflict preaching of the literate pulpit. It is too guarded to speak in apocalyptic terms. But it does pit moral indignation against sleazy life commitments and peace of mind against worldly success. Although its dualism is a limited one, it does manage to solicit the interest of the congregation along such lines, particularly if the terms are quite personal and the illustrations vivid.

Ideally, the interest in a sermon is borne by a fusion of biblical apocalyptic with modern pastoral psychology. The one deepens the perspective of preaching, so that its roots are firmly entrenched in the New Testament vision, and the other adjusts the focus to daily living, so that faith is applied to real problems instead of siphoning off people into indolent enclaves waiting for the end of the world. The fused version thus supports action in the temporal arena and views Christian commitment in terms of evangelical missions, education, economic and ecological reform, corporate reclamation, Third World development, and all the other frontline activities of faith. When this vision captures a minister's attention, the minister will not have much trouble capturing the attention of a congregation.

5. *Learn the effective art of repeating yourself.* One of the first things we learn in a writing or speaking course is to avoid repetition. "Say what you have to say and move on," advise the textbooks. "People grow weary when you repeat yourself." In general, that is good advice. There should be continual freshness in both spoken and written communication, as though the stream of thought were being constantly fed by new tributaries all along the way.

But there is another side to the coin. We have said in an earlier chapter that a sermon should have a single thrust — that everything in it should be gathered toward one great impression we hope to leave with the congregation. Actually there is no more effective technique for imprinting an idea in the minds of the congregation than repetition. What we wish them to remember we must say again and again. The trick is to be repetitive without seeming to be so — to march the same idea by the audience time after time without their becoming tired of it.

There are two basic ways of doing this. One is simple *rhetorical* repetition, in which a phrase or a sentence becomes the recitative that is voiced again and again at various points of progression in the sermon. When this method is used, the words of the repeated phrase remain the same each time. In fact, it is important that they remain unchanged. The congregation must become familiar with them and greet them as old friends when they appear again. Martin Luther King, Jr.'s famous "I Have a Dream" sermon was structured in this way. King repeated the "I have a dream" phrase again and again, adding new material each time it was uttered. He planted it on every bit of high ground he traversed in getting to the conclusion of the sermon. No one who heard the sermon could ever forget it. It had been drilled into the unconscious.

The other method is *subtle* repetition. In this technique, identical words and phrases are seldom repeated, but ideas are repeated in numerous ways. The preacher, paraphrasing Mrs. Browning, soliloquizes: "How can I say this? Let me count the ways." The object is to reinforce the central thrust of the sermon again and again without appearing to restate the thesis. Then, at the end of the sermon, the preacher can gather the force of all the arguments and illustrations together, as though pulling on a drawstring, and say, "You see how everything I have been saying leads to this single conclusion." People can then go off holding to the drawstring and fit everything they have heard under the one impression left by the sermon.

Some preachers, being instinctive orators, do not need to be told the importance of repetition. But most of us, for whom preaching is an acquired art, can bear the reminder. We are so prone to wish to cover a lot of ground in our sermons that we often fail to secure the bit of ground we have gained and let it slip away as soon as the after-sermon hymn is begun. Or, to change the metaphor, we watch the people lose all the pearls we have so patiently strung for them because we neglected to tie some strong knots in the string along the way.

Charles Finney, the noted evangelist, quoted in his autobiography what a justice of the Supreme Court once said to him about repetition. "Ministers," said the judge, "do not exercise good sense in addressing the people. They are afraid of repetition. Now, if lawyers should take such a course, they would ruin themselves and their cause. When I was at the bar, I used to take it for granted, when I had before me a jury of respectable men, that I should have to repeat over my main positions about as many times as there were persons in the jury-box. I learned that unless I did so, illustrated, and repeated, and turned the main points over — the main points of law and of evidence — I should lose my cause."

"We should all preach more effectively," said R. W. Dale, who had just quoted the passage above, "if, instead of tasking our intellectual resources to say a great many things in the same sermon, we tried to say a very few things in a great many ways."[10]

FROM MANUSCRIPT TO PULPIT

It should be evident, from merely talking about matters of style, how important the discipline of writing is to the preacher. Only in the written draft of the sermon can all these matters be carefully attended to; if we preach spontaneously, without written preparation, we can afterward only lament our failure to attend to them. And even then we shall do so only if we have tape-recorded our sermons and are willing to study them intently for errors in method. If we write, and write thoughtfully, we cannot but grow in our homiletical ability through the years.

But suppose we write out all our sermons, taking care to improve our methods as we go. We see a certain style emerging in our approach to preaching. What about the delivery of the sermon? Isn't that part of style too?

It is indeed, and how we get from the completed manuscript to the actual delivery of the sermon affects not only how other people perceive our styles but how we ourselves perceive them. That is, not only are our methods of preparing to preach determined by our personalities, but they *affect* our personalities. They make a difference in how we feel about preaching, and that in turn makes a difference in how we feel about ourselves as preachers. So this aspect of style is both tricky and important for us.

There is no single style of delivery, just as there is no single style of sermon composition. Each of the following methods has had its famous adherents and is worthy of consideration in the light of your own personal gifts and style of working:

1. *Reading.* There is one obvious advantage to this method: the preacher can give everything that was written word for word, so that nothing is forgotten and omitted, and can sleep well on Saturday night, confident of having a manuscript to depend on the next day. Those who have read their sermons have been quick to insist, however, that one must prepare well for the task of reading. Henry Sloane Coffin, who liked to read his sermons in order to be precise in preaching, said that he familiarized himself with the manuscript so that he could preach "through it"— presumably meaning that then the manuscript constituted no barrier between him and his audience.

The primary objection to the reading of sermons is that the manuscript does tend to be a barrier, requiring the preacher's attention when he or she should be making eye contact with the congregation. Spurgeon once likened preachers who read their sermons to hens drinking water — the up-and-down motions of the heads struck him as appearing comical. There is probably more reason to read sermons in large, cathedral churches, where most of the people are beyond the eye range of the minister anyway and the minister would have difficulty feeling conversational with the crowd. Fosdick eventually abandoned extemporaneous preaching and read his sermons at Riverside, convinced that nothing was lost in the process. "Speaking from an outline has been my most common practice," he said. "But in recent years I have found that one can have the full manuscript in front of him and can read it as though he were not reading but talking, with just as much freedom, spontaneity, colloquial directness, and person-to-person impact as though no manuscript were on the pulpit. Just as one can *write* for listeners, so one can *read* for listeners, combining the advantage of a manuscript's careful preparation with the freedom of face-to-face address."[11]

Edmund Holt Linn, a professor of speech who has made a comprehensive study of Fosdick's preaching, concludes, however, that Fosdick's use of the manuscript did not leave him as free, spontaneous, and direct as he liked to believe he was. His natural vivacity was much less in evidence when he read his sermons. Anyone who both heard him preach and knew him personally realized at once that he did not preach as he talked.[12]

2. *Memorizing.* Some preachers, blessed with near-photographic memories, have favored the complete memorization of their sermons. This was a popular method in the nineteenth century, when preaching was often treated as a kind of oratory. R. W. Dale, in his biography of John Angell James, says that he once heard James preach a two-hour sermon from memory without missing a word in his manuscript. At the close of the first hour, James asked the congregation's permission to pause for a few minutes. They sang a hymn, and then James preached for another hour.

Adam Burnet, minister of St. Cuthbert's in Edinburgh, followed the memorization method in all of his pulpit work. In his first charge, he said, it took him only an hour or two to master his weekly sermon. As he grew older, it took considerably longer. "It was memorizing," he said, "but not mere memorizing. It became more and more an assimilation of the whole thing until one was 'soaked' in it, the words not too hard to recall because written with care, but more and more the thoughts in their sequence laying hold of one, till the fire kindled all over again and by the grace of God the sermon began to glow with reality."[13]

Delivering the sermon from memory has one key advantage over reading, and that is that it permits the preacher to maintain eye contact with the congregation. There is no visible manuscript between speaker and audience—no *visible* manuscript. But therein is one of the problems. Some preachers who have memorized their scripts simply cannot deliver them naturally. They appear to be reading their sermons either from the back of their own minds or off giant cue cards behind the heads of the congregation. Their concentration is on the recovery of the manuscript in its exact wording, not upon responses from the people before them. They are not free, when there is an expression of puzzlement on faces in the audience, to stop and explain their meaning or to recover the ground in other words.

The greatest barrier to memorization, however, is the prodigious effort it requires. Most busy pastors simply do not have the time to write their sermons out and then spend a full day getting them by memory. Or, if they do take the time, they must compress their schedules for other things—visiting, counseling, personal study and refreshment—into such narrow space that they invariably feel harried and neglectful of their ministries.

3. *Extemporizing.* Probably the most popular method among preachers who take their craft seriously, extemporaneous preaching combines the primary advantages of a prepared manuscript with maximal freedom at the time of delivery. The preacher can still give full attention to the preparation of the sermon, getting the introduction just right, making sure the transitions are well worded, testing the balance of illustrative material, and generally seeing that the content and language are vigorous and interesting. Then, instead of memorizing the sermon, he or she merely reads

through it a few times, becoming very familiar with the way it is put together. (This sounds foolish to anyone who has not had the experience, but no creative person ever has a complete grasp on something on which he or she has just completed work.) Next, the preacher makes a brief outline of the manuscript, noting especially the ideas or transitions he or she deems most important to remember when preaching. This outline will be different from the one that preceded the writing of the sermon, for the sermon will have grown and changed in the process of composition. Then the preacher takes this outline to the pulpit and preaches from it, drawing both on remembered parts of the finished sermon and on native ingenuity and inspiration at the moment of preaching.

Preachers who employ this method often wince, on rereading their manuscripts after the service, to discover that they left out some particularly eloquent phrases or even some brief but telling illustrations when they delivered their sermons. But overall, their sermons were probably not that much poorer for it, because they undoubtedly also added some vital phrases and ideas as they preached that had not occurred to them when they were composing the manuscripts. And they had the distinct advantage, in delivery, of being able to speak conversationally to the people, responding to the various kinds of feedback that occur in the preaching situation.

It is important, if one uses this method of delivery, to complete the written sermon by Thursday evening or Friday morning in order to permit time for the familiarization process. David H. C. Read says that he normally finishes writing by noon on Friday. He reads over the manuscript that afternoon, and again on Saturday, time permitting. Then on Saturday night he gives it a serious reading, attempting to see the sermon as a whole and to be able to reconstruct it in his mind. He does not try to memorize it, only to see it in its general shape. On Sunday morning he gives it a final reading and rethinks it all as he walks to church.

In the pulpit, says Read, the preacher needs to experience the freedom of the Spirit. The manuscript, whose meticulousness of preparation has provided a necessary discipline of thought and language, cannot be allowed to interfere.

In human terms, the sermon must now come alive. No matter how much toil and sweat has gone into the preparation, it must now be spoken with direct contact and immediacy. That means an actual rethinking in the presence of a congregation of what was laboriously worked over on paper. There must be no impression of the second-hand, of repetition of something which has already been done. This rules out straight reading, whether from a manuscript or from some point in the back of a memorizer's mind. Like an actor, the preacher has to be sensitive to his audience, knowing instinctively when they are following or when he has lost them, when they are alert and when they are tired, and he must be ready to change pace, repeat, or pause, according to the mood.[14]

John Redhead, minister of First Presbyterian Church in Greensboro, North Carolina, carefully wrote out every sermon he preached. Then, having familiarized himself with it, he refused to take the manuscript or even any notes into the pulpit on the grounds that "paper is said to be a poor conductor of heat." He wanted to focus his entire attention on the congregation during the time of delivery.

A PSYCHOLOGICAL MATTER

One thing that greatly affects how a preacher delivers the sermon is the way the preacher feels about his or her relationship to the congregation. If there is a sense of trust toward the congregation, an understanding that the congregation is loving and supportive, the preacher feels much freer in mind and spirit to preach well. If not, the preacher may feel unbearably constricted in delivery. A preacher addressing a very formal congregation in a cathedral setting may experience such spiritual isolation that he or she feels bound to a manuscript for preaching. The same preacher, delivering the same sermon before a congregation in a cozy little village church, may throw away the manuscript and preach enthusiastically without even a note.

One of the phenomena associated with the ministry is something I have called "the preacher's dream." Every preacher has it, sooner or later. It takes many forms, but basically it is an apprehensive dream about being unprepared to preach. Sometimes the preacher sees himself or herself in the pulpit without any clothes or in the worst possible state of dress. Sometimes the preacher has forgotten his or her sermon notes, or has brought the wrong sermon, one that was preached in that congregation the previous Sunday. Invariably there is a great deal of anxiety associated with the dream. The preacher does not need an analyst to understand that the anxiety is real even when the dream is false—that he or she feels a basic insecurity about the weekly task of standing before an audience and trying to preach an acceptable sermon.

At times when the anxiety level is high, preaching is difficult. The strain on the preacher's personality inhibits a free flow of thought and delivery. It may help at such times to confess this strain to the congregation—to appeal for the kind of personal support that will ease the tension and permit the preacher to feel uninhibited again. The anxiety is also a sign that the preacher has been neglecting his or her self in important ways—that there has been too little time spent in prayer and quiet reflection, or too little time with the family, or too little time laughing and having fun with friends. When the preacher's self-concept is strong, there is more freedom for preaching. When it is weak, the anxieties return.

Ideally, in the Christian community there is such an abundance of love and goodwill that the preacher can always speak out of a feeling of overflow, not underflow. If the preacher is having to strain to preach, and sometimes actually dreads the hour of worship when the preaching will occur, it is a sign of spiritual crisis either in the minister or in the entire congregation. The cure for it is not in more attention to the preaching but in a deeper care for the life of the spirit. When the sense of community joy is high, the preacher should feel free enough to preach without a manuscript—or, for that matter, *with* a manuscript—and not be inhibited by fears of not performing well. Performance is, after all, a sub-Christian ideal; in Christ, we are loved for who we are, not for what we do.

Many preachers find it helpful, both in preparing and in delivering sermons, to keep in mind specific persons in the congregation. This creates a warm psychological bond between preacher and audience and assures that the sermon is more than a vaporous exercise concocted on Thursday for dissipation in the pulpit on Sunday. Others have found it helpful to pray for certain persons in the congregation before preaching the sermon, that they may hear something in it to lift their souls or ease a time of crisis. Fosdick said in his autobiography that his invariable prayer before he entered the pulpit was, "Lord, somebody out there needs what I have to say this morning. Help me to get at him."

SUGGESTIONS ABOUT DELIVERY

As a professor of preaching, I never worried very much about my students' delivery; I was always far more concerned that they have something to say. If they had truly worked on the sermon, I reasoned, and were excited about their own messages, the messages would get through, regardless of any speech mannerisms or difficulties they might have. In general, I believe that is true. The dedicated preacher, on the other hand, is right to be concerned about effectiveness in communicating the sermon. Even a person who calls trains in a depot needs to be clear and audible. Phillips Brooks, after he became master of Trinity pulpit in Boston, took voice lessons from a teacher in Cambridge, eager to improve the instrument God had given him. There are few of us who could not sharpen our skills at communication if we were that willing to work at the job.

The minister who is really interested in a course of self-improvement in this area is advised to put himself or herself in the care of a competent teacher of speech for a least a refresher course in the use of the voice, the manner of gesturing, and the natural composure of the body during vocal communication. With the advent of videotaping, it is possible for the eager student to learn a great deal about communicating in a very short time, and there are few who make the effort who do not think it is time well spent.

For the moment, let me suggest three simple things about the delivery of the sermon that apply generally to all preachers.

1. *Preach naturally.* Remember, preaching is truth through personality—*your* personality. Therefore you should avoid any mannerisms in speech or posture that are not you, that you have acquired from watching and hearing other speakers. Such man-

nerisms not only misrepresent who you are, they actually inhibit your true manners from coming out as you preach. I remember a country minister I met when he was preaching one Saturday night years ago. He was a "whooping" minister—one of those rural preachers who learn to suck in great volumes of air between phrases, making a rhythmical, rasping noise that becomes almost mesmeric as they talk. Not only that, he had acquired a most unusual manner of swinging his hips and taking a little jump to the side every sentence or two—first to the left and then to the right. I can't recall a thing he said—I doubt if anyone else could— but I shall never forget the experience of witnessing his performance. He whooped and jumped, jumped and whooped, for nearly an hour. He was exhausted when the service ended. When I had met the man before the service, I noted that he had a most winsome way of smiling at you when he spoke, and that he had a very pleasant, well-modulated voice. Neither of these attributes was in evidence as he preached. The whooping and jumping kept him so thoroughly occupied that he had no opportunity either to smile at us or to use his voice pleasantly. His fake mannerisms, acquired from heaven knows where, completely overrode his real personality, so that we never had the advantage of it. That is an extreme case, but the same problem is often in evidence in less extreme forms. Every preacher should examine himself or herself to see that delivery of the sermon is consonant with daily personality and behavior.

In former times, many preachers developed oratorical manners of speaking out of sheer necessity: without amplifying systems, something had to be done to increase the projecting power of the human voice. Today, with sensitive and relatively inexpensive amplifiers, there is no need for such affected voices. The ideal of speech is heard in the normal, almost conversational, tones of the evening news broadcast. For preachers to persist in using artificial patterns of inflection and abnormal volume is to mark the church as an anachronistic society, frozen in the never-never world of some previous era. We should speak to a congregation as we would to an intimate group of friends—raising and lowering the voice naturally, gesturing for emphasis as the body normally moves to sculpt the pictures it is seeing, and generally behaving as though we were sane, healthy, and emotionally sound human beings. That way the gospel is more credible in the age in which we live. It is being heard through our personalities, not through some fabricated personalities that we stand in the pulpit for twenty minutes on Sunday morning.

2. *Preach animatedly.* The word "animated" is from the Latin *anima*, meaning "soul." Preach with soul. Preach as though you were alive, as though you yourself were responsive to the word you have to give to the congregation. I have heard preachers speak as if they were so bored it was all they could do to endure their own sermons to the end. That is a disgraceful response to the gospel. The gospel should quicken us to life—make us more sensitive to flowers and clouds and buildings, more aware of children and widows and people with tension in their faces. To preach without animation is to give up the game before it is played. It says, in effect, none of what I am saying to you has made much difference in my own case; I am either hopelessly uptight or hopelessly apathetic about everything.

The degree of animation should of course be suited to the content of the sermon at the moment we are preaching it. That way there will be an agreeable variety of pace and emphasis in our delivery. It is not "soul" when one turns on animation at the wrong time. Colin Morris speaks in *The Word and the Words* about preachers who perform "as though they were announcing the end of the world when the *content* of their sermon makes the London telephone directory in contrast seem charged with the power of God," and of preachers, on the other hand, who proclaim the imminent end of the world "with all the vivacity of a radio announcer reciting vegetable prices at Covent Garden."[15] We are here again in the province of what it means to be natural or unnatural and to preach in a voice commensurate with the meaning of the material in our sermons.

But more preachers err, I believe, on the side of too little animation than on the side of too much. Often they go into their pulpits on Sunday morning tired from too many trivial duties the week before and burdened with a feeling of inadequate preparation for the hour at hand. Their spirits are downcast. However glibly they assert that the gospel of Christ is a gospel of joy and celebration, their body language and tone of voice say differently. There is a drabness in their manner that infects everything they say, every gesture they make. The message they broadcast most loudly is, "I'll be glad when this is over."

The preacher's mood, like the mood of the music and worship generally, is contagious. If it is dour and sullen, the mood of the congregation will be dull and heavy. If it is lively and bright, the mood of the congregation will be correspondingly happy. It is especially important, therefore, that the minister be in touch with the deeper resources of faith as he or she gets up to preach, so that the sermon will convey an appropriate subliminal message to the congregation.

R. W. Dale has told that, one Easter Day, he felt sodden and lethargic about preaching. He was a busy preacher and pastor, and the months had taken a heavy toll on his spirit. But as he paced his study floor before the hour of worship, wishing he did not have to go into the pulpit at all, the realization suddenly struck him with great force: "Christ is alive! Christ is alive!" Even if he had not had the realization, Dale would surely have preached that message to his congregation that morning. But suddenly his vision of what he had to do was transformed. He no longer felt tired and lethargic. Instead, he was eager to preach, to tell people that Christ's resurrection makes all the difference in their lives. He felt the difference in his own life. And when he went into the pulpit that morning, he spoke with a freshness and animation that were discernible to all. It was not only the words he said that counted, it was the glint in his eye, the smile on his face, the ring of certainty in his voice. He preached "over his head," as we say.

And so should every preacher who has been with Christ.

3. *Finally, preach responsively.* Watch the congregation. See and feel their reactions. Preach to those reactions. Lighten your tone when they find the going too heavy. Deepen it when they are smiling and in a good mood. Play to their needs and feelings as if you were a skilled actor or musician, sensitive to the invisible strands joining you to them in a great communal enterprise.

Harold Schonberg, music critic for the *New York Times*, has said of Arthur Rubinstein, the famous pianist, that he plays his audience as well as the music; Rubinstein, says Schonberg, has "a platform personality that comes over the footlights and caresses everyone in the auditorium." This is what the truly gifted preacher does — caresses everyone in the auditorium. The preacher watches the eyes, the tilt of the faces, the position of the bodies, and programs all of these things into the way the sermon is preached — not consciously, of course, but unconsciously. It is like making love to the congregation. That is what William Self, the senior minister of Wieuca Road Baptist Church in Atlanta, says that preaching is for him — "twenty minutes to love the congregation."

This is a situation for which the extemporaneous method of preaching seems to offer advantages over either reading or memorizing the sermon. The preacher who knows the sense of the sermon but is free from the slavish use of what has been written can respond instantly to the mood of the congregation — can repeat something that was not understood, can omit something that doesn't seem to fit the present temper of things, can introduce humor or pathos or whatever is immediately called for.

I remember the occasion when James Stewart of Scotland and D. T. Niles of Sri Lanka (then Ceylon) were both scheduled to preach for several days at Princeton University, honoring the 150th anniversary of the school. I had never heard of D. T. Niles, but I had read Stewart's books for years, and I eagerly awaited his coming. Donald Macleod, professor of preaching at Princeton Theological Seminary, introduced Stewart as "the man whose illustrations adorn all our sermons." It seemed an apt way to greet the great man from Edinburgh. Stewart climbed the pulpit steps, opened his manuscript and began to read his sermon. He read well, and the sermon was a typical Stewart sermon, grounded in the New Testament, clearly outlined, and memorably illustrated. I was impressed. Out of curiosity, I returned to the chapel an hour later to hear Niles. He was a short, round-faced man with brown skin and with a shock of black hair falling across his forehead. His suit was ill-fitting and looked as if he had slept in it. I suppose he was properly introduced, though I cannot now recall the introduction. I only remember feeling sorry for him as he climbed into the pulpit without a manuscript. "To have to follow James Stewart!" I thought, and knew I wouldn't wish to do it. But something happened when Niles got into the pulpit. He acted as if it weren't there at all. He began talking to us so casually and conversationally that we weren't aware he was preaching. Stories tumbled out, humorous remarks, stunning insights. Looking back, I realize the sermon had to have been written in advance, but the man made no effort to get every word precisely as it had been on paper. He knew what he wanted to say, but the important thing was the way he played the congregation. His timing was as perfect as a good comedian's. He knew when to be funny and when to be serious. He was as responsive to our reactions as if he had been a lumberjack at the other end of a crosscut saw, pulling at his end in perfect rhythm with the way we pulled at ours. He did the same thing every time he preached. By the end of the week everyone idolized him. Stewart continued to preach his excellent manuscripts. But they seemed somehow artificial and literary beside the robust sermons of Niles. When Stewart preached, we were always conscious of listening to a preacher. When Niles preached, we were enraptured. We saw new visions of life. We felt the presence of God. I have never, in the years since, felt justified in using a manuscript when I preached. Niles, I am convinced, was the ultimate. He made something with the congregation. He didn't just make it in the study and then set it before the congregation. He made it with the people. Part of what went into his sermons was provided by the congregation.

Ideally, we should all preach that way.

NOTES

1. George A. Buttrick, *Jesus Came Preaching* (New York: Charles Scribner's Sons, 1931), p. 159.
2. Herbert H. Farmer, *The Servant of the Word* (London: Nisbet and Co., 1941), p. 102.

3. Malcolm Cowley, ed., *Writers at Work: The Paris Review Interviews* (New York: Viking Press, 1959), p. 146.

4. Henry Ward Beecher, *Lectures on Preaching* (New York: J. B. Ford and Co., 1872), vol. 1, p. 131.

5. James S. Stewart, *Heralds of God: A Practical Book on Preaching* (New York: Charles Scribner's Sons, 1956), p. 152.

6. Colin Morris, *The Word and the Words* (London: Epworth Press, 1975), p. 57.

7. Reuel L. Howe, *Partners in Preaching: Clergy and Laity in Dialogue* (New York: Seabury Press, 1967), p. 29.

8. A. J. Gossip, *In Christ's Stead* (London: Hodder & Stoughton, 1925), p. 64.

9. Gene Bartlett, *The Audacity of Preaching* (New York: Harper & Brothers, 1962), p. 51.

10. R. W. Dale, *Nine Lectures on Preaching* (New York: Barnes, 1878), pp. 149–150.

11. Harry Emerson Fosdick, "How I Prepare My Sermons," *The Quarterly Journal of Speech* 40, no. 1 (February 1954):289.

12. Edmund Holt Linn, *Preaching as Counseling: The Unique Method of Harry Emerson Fosdick* (Valley Forge, Pa.: Judson Press, 1966), pp. 148–49.

13. In Robert J. Smithson, ed., *My Way of Preaching* (London: Pickering and Inglis, n.d.), p. 29.

14. David H. C. Read, *Sent from God* (Nashville: Abingdon Press, 1974), p. 110.

15. Morris, *The Word and the Words*, p. 119.

---8---

What to
Preach

"To write a mighty book," said Herman Melville in a preface to *Moby Dick*, "you must have a mighty theme."

Christian preachers do have a mighty theme—how God has acted in Christ to give us wholeness of life in the eternal family—and it is important that our sermons embody that theme. There is nothing more trivial than preaching that misses it. Ministers are called to preach the gospel, not offer commentary on what is happening to hairdos and hemlines. When people come to us, said Barth,

> they do not really want to learn more about *living*: they want to learn more about what is on the farther edge of living—*God*. We cut a ridiculous figure as village sages—or city sages. As such we are socially superfluous. We do not understand the profession of the ministry unless we understand it as an index, a symptom, say rather an omen, of a perplexity which extends over the whole range of human endeavor, present and future.[1]

P. T. Forsyth expressed a similar concern when he said: "There is even less room for originality of idea in the pulpit than elsewhere. What is needed is rather spontaneity of power . . . to assist the Church to a fresh appropriation of its own gospel."[2]

It is human to stray from the great central matters of life. One day during the deliberations of a Vatican II committee meeting in a Paris hotel to debate the shape of the pall, a small cloth laid over the chalice in Communion services, there was such a ruckus outside that one of the bishops ordered the window shutters closed.

The noise outside was the Student Revolution of 1968. The bishops were arguing about the shape of a cloth while students were tearing up paving stones and hurling them at police. And George Sweazey reminds us that George III, on the eve of the American Revolution, regaled the English Parliament with a disquisition on the health of cattle.[3]

Ministers often do as badly. We carry some inadequate homily about textual matters or ecclesiastical etiquette before a congregation of people who are battling loneliness and fear, worrying about jobs and education, trying to hold on to crumbling marriages, and facing death. We stand before desperate people and offer them pious platitudes about religious symbolism and the history of the faith. It is no wonder the church in our day often seems to lack power. When the gospel is not heard from the pulpit, there is nothing to unify the hearts of the people. They go away as confused and forlorn as they came.

"Glorious is the song," said Christopher Smart, the eighteenth-century poet, "when God's the theme." No preacher should settle for a lesser theme. As long as we tell the story of God's activities of redemption, especially in Jesus Christ, we remain true to our calling. When we stray from this subject, our very ministries start to deteriorate.

THE NEED FOR VARIETY

Still, preachers are expected to vary the way they present the word of God's wooing. Messages that are habitual and predictable soon become trite and boring. As soon as they are begun, people shift their minds into neutral and begin to daydream about other things. The two-edged sword becomes a plastic butter knife. The gospel does not really become interfaced with human predicaments, and people leave the service of worship hungry for revelation.

The preacher who has nothing fresh to say each Sunday is failing to stay mentally and spiritually alert through the week. There is no special trick to infusing variety into one's preaching. It is simply a matter of being alive, of staying interested in things, of listening to people, of reflecting on the way the gospel continues to work in the world around us. Some preachers appear to have died the day they were ordained. Their minds became frozen at the point where they were. Thus everything they know about life and the gospel has become a cliché, a threadbare thought or phrase they merely repeat again and again when they enter the pulpit to preach or pray. This is inexcusable. It is like a doctor's failing to stay abreast of developments in medicine, or a poet's failing to have any fresh thoughts, or a musician's failing to master any new compositions. When there is no dedication to growth, no encounter with new material or situations, the brain atrophies. Performance becomes automatic — and unreal.

The greatest preachers have always been those who stayed closest to the central theme of ministry — the saving work of God — yet managed to clothe that theme in an infinite variety of modes. Spurgeon rarely got more than a stone's throw from the theme, yet treated such a variety of subjects that people rode the train to London from all parts of England to secure his latest sermons. Fosdick never wavered in his fidelity to the theme, yet no two of his sermons ever sounded alike. Buttrick preached for more than fifty years, always sounding the theme like a high call from a minaret, and even when he was eighty years old other preachers were still coming to his audiences to write down the fresh and pungent things he had to say.

James Stewart is right — faithfulness to the theme and the achievement of creative variety do not exclude each other. "I am insisting on what is paradoxical but true," he says, "that the more resolutely and stubbornly you refuse to be deflected from the one decisive theme, the greater the variety you will achieve; while the more you seek variety by wandering from your centre, the faster the descent to bathos and monotony. God's deed in Christ touches life at every point. It speaks to every aspect of the human predicament."[4]

What is required is that we remain sensitive to the way the gospel confronts each new situation around us and how it is constantly taking new language to define its relationship to life. As Gerhard von Rad has pointed out, modern poets have had to find new words to express the tensions and feelings of existence in our time; with the old words, they could only duplicate the emotions of an earlier age.[5] The faithful preacher also struggles to find language capable of expressing the gospel in a new era. He or she weighs and tests the gospel in terms of current experience, so that the history of faith has its creative life in our own time. Those who are content merely to duplicate the words and phrases of preachers in centuries gone by are not living at the spiritual center of life. Their speech is but an echo of where Christians have been and what they have thought in the past. It lacks the vibrancy of a living language.

There is a Zen parable about a certain master who was asked to define the meaning of Zen. The master, in the absurd fashion of a true roshi, merely lifted his index finger against the sky. Later, a report came to the master that one of his disciples, whenever a villager asked him to define the meaning of Zen, was imitating the master and holding up his index finger. The master ordered the disciple to him. Laying the disciple's hand on a chopping block, he lopped off the the index finger. "Now," he demanded of the terrified disciple, "tell me the meaning of Zen."

We achieve true variety in our preaching when we refuse merely to preach what others have preached before us — when we resolve to experience the presence of God in our own lives and to preach out of that experience. Then the central theme of our preaching continues to be heard in new language and metaphor, and people realize that faith is a living process, not an empty profession.

PLANNING YOUR PULPIT WORK

At the practical level, variety in preaching is encouraged by preplanning our sermon emphases well in advance, so that we can have an overview of the subjects and accents in time to remedy them if we need to. Ministers who follow the lectionary in selecting sermon texts have their work of planning largely done. Yet even they need to give attention to matters of subject and emphasis, lest they manage to find essentially the same ideas in many of the texts and end by striking more or less the same note in every sermon. The work of the Holy Spirit is not impeded by such planning; it is actually enhanced. When we are free from the anxiety of wondering what we shall preach from week to week, we can follow the Spirit's leading without constriction. It is the minister who has not planned well—the minister who comes to Thursday without the certainty of a text or a theme for the sermon needed on Sunday—who is suddenly blocked from hearing the Spirit's voice.

Andrew Blackwood in *Planning a Year's Pulpit Work* advocated what his title suggests—outlining one's preaching an entire year in advance. Others have suggested that a more modest range is desirable—say, half a year, or even a quarter. Life moves so quickly now, they say, and moods change so precipitously, that it is impossible to project accurately the needs for an entire year. Be that as it may, there is obvious advantage to preplanning one's work, even for as short a period as a quarter of a year. And if one uses the Christian calendar as a basis for much of the planning, there is no reason that one cannot sketch in, at least rudimentarily, at least six months' worth of pulpit emphases.

Blackwood liked the idea of outlining a year's work at a time because he understood the need for the preacher's having some relaxed days in which to do the planning. He recommended using vacation time for this exercise. Away from the pressures of daily ministry, the average minister's mind becomes more reflective and creative. Like a ship loosed from its tether, it heads for deeper waters, calls in at strange ports, and generally has a more unobstructed view of the horizon. In this situation, Blackwood felt, it is natural for the minister to begin ruminating about the months ahead and to arrive, without any sense of tension or pressure, at a relatively clear picture of what needs to be done. Many ministers corroborate this intuition. They are at their most creative, they say, during the second and third weeks of their vacation month. Lying on a beach by the ocean, standing knee-deep in a cold trout stream, or watching a golf ball sail beautifully down a long fairway, they see the vistas of their future work open before them with unparalleled clarity and insight.

What is accomplished by this kind of projection is what George Gibson calls "the grand architecture of the year."[6] The year's pulpit work rises, not higgledy-piggledy, like a house thrown up by a small child, but rationally and soundly, like a building constructed by a master architect, who understands the principles of balance, stress, support, and design.

THE CHRISTIAN YEAR

The best place to begin one's planning, it is generally agreed, is with the Christian calendar. For many years, the free churches avoided this calendar as a vestige of popery. Our Puritan forebears did not even hold with the celebration of Christmas and Easter in the church. Every Lord's Day, they said, is the day of Resurrection, and annual celebrations only encourage spiritual slothfulness among the people. In the strictest sense, perhaps, they were right. But most people are not models of spiritual self-discipline, as the Puritan leaders were. They need the rhythm of special emphases to turn their minds and hearts to God. Today most Protestant churches follow at least a modified version of the Christian calendar, emphasizing major holy days, and many use a lectionary based on the calendar.

Beginning with Advent, the Christian calendar carries us through the central events in the life of Christ and the formation of the early church, then offers a season whose emphasis is on the human response to the gospel. In terms of "the grand architecture of the year," it offers an annual framework for teaching the faith through sermon and liturgy. If followed faithfully, it guarantees a kind of balance to the spiritual and doctrinal program of the congregation. Here are the primary accents of the Christian year:

Advent. The word "Advent," from the Latin words *ad venio,* meaning "to come to," designates the four Sundays before Christmas. The emphasis during these Sundays is on the coming of Christ. Traditionally, the first Sunday is known as "Creation" Sunday, the second as "Bible" Sunday, the third as "Prophets" Sunday, and the fourth as "Forerunner" Sunday or "John the Baptist" Sunday. Many ministers try to plan their pulpit themes around these topics, while at the same time focusing on the incarnation and the Second Coming of Christ.

Christmastide. The Sunday or Sundays following Christmas Day are known as Christmastide. As Albert Mollegen has written: "The accent of Advent is preparation for the coming of Christ on the basis of the first coming. The accent of Christmastide is the *receiving* of Christ on the basis of his having come."[7] Many preachers have used their sermons on the Sunday after Christmas to stress the importance of keeping the Christmas spirit alive through the year ahead. Some titles of such sermons are "The Post-Christmas Blues," "Making Christmas Last," "Taking Jesus Into Egypt," and "When the Star Has Gone."

Epiphany. The day of Epiphany, sometimes called Old Christmas, is January 6. It is the day associated with the visit of the Magi to see and worship the Christ-child and therefore reminds us of the universalism of the gospel or the good news for the Gentiles. Epiphany season may last up to six Sundays. It features emphases from the prophets, Gospels, and epistles on the universal or cosmic Christ. The preacher may preach a sermon, for example, on Isa. 60:3, "The nations shall march towards thy light and their kings towards the brightness of thy rising." It is also a good season for an emphasis on missions, because Christ's universal kingdom is ushered in by the preaching of the gospel in all lands.

Pre-Lent. There are three Sundays of pre-Lenten observance, sometimes known by their Latin names of Septuagesima, Sexagesima, and Quinquagesima. How many of them are observed in a particular year depends on how early Easter comes. If Easter is very early, the calendar may move directly from the Epiphany season into Lent. Because Pre-Lent serves merely as a bridge between two more important seasons, it is little emphasized in Protestantism. But the Sundays may serve as an occasion for preaching one to three sermons on a pre-Lenten theme, such as the need for humility or self-understanding.

Lent. Beginning on Ash Wednesday, forty days before Easter (excluding Sundays), Lent is the traditional period of greatest devotion and reconsecration in the Christian year. The name is derived from the Anglo-Saxon *lencten*, or "spring," which originally applied to the lengthening of the days after winter. Medieval piety reached its zenith during this period. People often underwent extreme fasting, and lack of nourishment sometimes induced visions and hallucinations among them. It was also a time of intense study and learning for new converts, in preparation for their baptism into the faith on Easter Day. Lent is still a time of reexamination for many Christians, and preaching during this season often raises questions about our loyalty and commitment to Christ. It is a good time for series of sermons on prayer and the devotional life, on the relationship between belief and action, and on the meaning of discipleship. Many preachers have used it as a season to preach on the Ten Commandments or the Sermon on the Mount.

Holy Week. Beginning with Palm Sunday, commemorating Jesus' royal entrance into Jerusalem, and climaxing with Good Friday and Easter Day, this week of special emphasis highlights the final events in the life and ministry of Christ. Monday recalls the cleansing of the Temple, Tuesday the controversies with the Pharisees, Wednesday the withdrawal into Bethany, Thursday the night in the upper room, and Friday the crucifixion. As Advent constitutes a psychological preparation for the remembrance of Christmas, this week helps people to prepare for the remembrance of the crucifixion and the resurrection, two of the most important events in the life of Christ. Only the most unimaginative of ministers could not think of many possibilities for preaching individual sermons or series of sermons at this time. Recalling the seven last words of Jesus is a favorite schema. Howard Hageman has given an excellent treatment of this theme in the meditations that constitute his book *We Call This Friday Good.* Another favorite framework is a series of sermons on the people involved with Jesus at the end of his life. Leslie Weatherhead, for example, published an excellent collection of sermons entitled *Personalities of the Passion* — biographical sermons dealing with such persons as Peter, John, Mary, Pilate, and the centurion.

Easter Day and Eastertide. Easter Day, celebrating the resurrection of Christ, is the climax of the entire Christian year. It is unthinkable that on this day the preacher should preach on any theme but the resurrection. People are excited about the resurrection and life after death. It is almost as if some mystical tide, having flowed underground for months, suddenly rises and floods through the congregation at this time. The preacher need not resort to arguments for the plausibility of Jesus' resurrection or the immortality of the soul. It is a time instead to declare the power of God to triumph over death and the grave. We do not establish the tide; we merely sail in on it! With Ps. 29:10 as a text—"The Lord sitteth upon the flood; yea, the Lord sitteth King for ever"— one might even wish to preach on "The King of the Flood." Eastertide, which covers the intervening weeks until Ascension Day, is a season for continuing the resurrection emphasis and applying it to the lives of our people, the church, and the world.

Ascension Sunday. This Sunday follows Ascension Day, which is always the fifth Thursday after Easter. It was originally known as Expectation Sunday, signaling the beginning of the period when the apostles were looking forward to the coming of the Holy Spirit at Pentecost. Little is made today of the doctrine of the ascension of Christ, for our scientific mind-set does not readily accept the picture of Christ floating off to heaven and leaving the apostles below, waving like a band of merry followers watching their leader go off in a balloon. But, coupled with the expectation theme, this is a good time to preach about the cosmic Christ and what it means for his Spirit to be abroad in the world.

Pentecost Sunday. Pentecost occurs seven weeks after Easter. As a Jewish festival, it marks the end of the reaping season, just as Passover marks the beginning. It is also associated, in Judaism, with the giving of the Law of Moses, which helped to unify the twelve tribes of Israel into a single nation. In Christianity, it is likewise associated with reaping, as it marked the first great ingathering of the church, and with unification, as the coming of the Spirit enabled all the strangers gathered in one place to understand each other as if they spoke in a common tongue. Pentecost completes the first half of the Christian year and serves as a bridge to the second half, when the emphasis shifts from what God has done in human history to what the church should be doing in response. It is a great time to celebrate the existence of the church and the presence of the Holy Spirit in the world. Sermon titles that have appeared for Pentecost include "What's a Nice Church Like You Doing in a World Like This?," "From Babel to Pentecost," "When the Message Became the Medium," "An Anniversary We Shouldn't Miss," and "The Power of a Unified Church."

Trinity Sunday. Preachers often recognize this Sunday, the first after Pentecost, by preaching on the nature of God. The Sunday also inaugurates the second half of the Christian year, in which it is proper to emphasize the Christian life and its various social, moral, ethical, and civic concerns. A doctrinal foundation for Christian faith has been laid during the first half of the year; now it is time to apply the faith to specific problems in the human arena and to think about the church's mission to the world. Whereas the first half of the year was spent thinking about Jesus, the second half is more devoted to what he taught and how that affects the way we live. Sermons will reflect Jesus' teachings about love, the kingdom, sacrifice, money, gifts, and numerous other subjects. Texts will often include material from the Sermon on the Mount, the parables, and the expansions of Jesus' teaching in the epistles and the Apocalypse.

ADDITIONS TO THE CALENDAR

Once one has entered into his or her preaching schedule all the special events of the Christian year, there are special events of the secular calendar to consider. For example, the preacher who misses the opportunity near the Fourth of July, or Independence Day, to speak about the relationship between God and country has neglected to treat an important subject at a time when people's hearts are most prepared to think about it. The thoughtful minister, in planning his or her preaching calendar, will list all the important secular holidays and reflect on the possibility of using people's sentiments at these times to deal with significant topics.

Mother's Day, Memorial Day, Father's Day, Labor Day, Halloween, Thanksgiving, all rank high in the holiday-conscious minds of our parishioners. To ignore them in our pulpit planning is to miss out on the natural contexts for applying the gospel in our people's lives.

The line must of course be drawn somewhere. As Gibson says: "While religion is said to be concerned with the whole of life, the connection seems tenuous when it comes to Paint Up Week or East Texas Yam Day; and while all good men may be expected to cooperate with Fire Prevention Week or Be Kind to Animals Day, it is hardly the function of the church to lead the crusade."[8] But whenever special emphases help us to enter into more effective communication with the people in the congregation, so that they understand the gospel of the kingdom in ways they never understood before, we would be foolish to ignore them.

What we have, then, is the calendar of the Christian year, with its dual emphasis on what God has done in Christ and what we must do now in response, with another calendar of secular holidays and emphases to be interwoven with it, providing a calendrical network for the year. Sermon possibilities for the various dates glitter on this network like dew on a spiderweb. Our preaching programs are already largely set for us. There is no need for feelings of despair about having so many occasions to preach and so few sermons with which to meet the occasions. The occasions themselves call forth many of the sermons.

SERIES PREACHING

A favorite technique of most experienced preachers is to plan series of sermons for special seasons such as Advent or Lent and also for the long stretches of Sundays in Pentecost or Kingdomtide. There are several advantages to planning sermons in a series, as opposed to planning them individually. First, there is more power in four sermons with a single focus than there is in one sermon. Second, there is more educational value in four sermons than there is in one. Third, the preacher's background of reading and psychological preparation for the homiletical task is utilized more economically in a series than in an individual sermon. Fourth, it is easier to write sermons in a series than sermons that must be approached singly; some preachers find that they can prepare the manuscripts for three or four sermons in a matter of two days, because the subject matter seems to unfold naturally and spontaneously. Fifth, in any series, the preacher probably does one or two sermons he or she wouldn't have done otherwise, and grows in the process. Sixth, it is easier to preach sermons in a series, because people build a residue of anticipation and excitement as the series moves along. Seventh, there is a sense of accomplishment about having preached a good series of sermons that is seldom there when sermons are considered as isolated entities.

Ordinarily, it is best to keep series relatively brief — perhaps six or seven sermons at the most. One minister is reported to have given a Sunday each to the twelve wells and threescore and ten palm trees of Elim. But people can tire of a series, especially one that is not very inspiring. A mini-series of three or four sermons is more likely to win favor for most subjects that have a topical flavor, such as "Contemporary Views of Death," "The Moral Climate of Our Times," or "Business Ethics and the Bible." Subject areas such as "The Ten Commandments Today" and "The Miracles of Jesus" naturally need a more extensive treatment, but even then it is probably wise to preach the series in two installments, treating other topics in the interim.

There is almost no limit to the number of topics that can be profitably preached in a series. The minister should periodically review the needs of the congregation, either with consultants or through a questionnaire inviting the congregation's suggestions, and design series to deal with the most important subjects. In Lent, for example, it is often desirable to feature a series on humility, penitence, or the devotional life. At a time when many Christians know very little about prayer and spirituality, the topic might be "Prayer and the Christian Life" or "Five Clues to Spiritual Living." A series during Holy Week, or on the Sundays immediately before Easter, might feature "The Significant Enemies Jesus Made." An Eastertide series could consider "Modern Evidences of Life After Death," a subject very much in keeping with the theme of Easter Day. In the summertime, when the emphasis of the Christian year is on our response to God's action in Christ, a series could be offered on "Christ and the Moral Crisis" or "The Church in the Twentieth Century."

It is important that ministers vary the emphases of their series so that people do not have the feeling that a sameness prevails in all of them. Attention can be given in one series to a theological accent, in another to biblical exposition, in another to devotional questions, and in yet another to ethical matters. By mapping out strategy several months in advance, the minister can resolve to shape each series according to an emphasis unique in recent preaching.

The series can be an especially effective method for preaching on the salient ideas of a book of the Bible. Some preachers assign themselves the task of doing this once a year in order to discipline themselves to new biblical study. They acquire the best commentaries on the particular book to be emphasized, begin the study a month or two in advance of planning the preaching, and mark out the main ideas or pericopes they intend to treat. By selecting wisely, they can easily preach through Amos, Hosea, Galatians, or Philippians in a brief series, or Jeremiah, Mark, Acts, or Romans in a longer series or split series.

The sermons in each series should have their individual autonomy, yet contribute to the larger picture of the entire series. Some persons in the congregation will be unable to hear all the sermons in a series; therefore each sermon should stand independently of the others in conveying its own message. But for persons hearing all the sermons there ought to be a line of continuity easy to grasp. Achieving this dual purpose in each sermon is not difficult if one simply plans all the sermons for the series — in rudimentary form — at the same time. This means sketching in titles, major thrusts, purposes of the sermons, and perhaps even texts and a few illustrations. Surprisingly, perhaps, this is not difficult to do. When ideas begin to flow, the entire series takes shape almost as easily as a single sermon does.

It is often desirable to print the messages of a series, even if the minister's sermons are not ordinarily published. Many people like to restudy what has been said, to examine points that were not entirely clear, and generally to refresh themselves on the major themes of a series.

BALANCING EMPHASES

The calendar itself provides a certain variety to preaching. But sensitive preachers will realize that a variety of mood or tone is also important if they are to speak to the varieties of personal mood and individual need in their congregations. If ministers are dull and unimaginative, their sermons will have a deadly sameness regardless of the superficial themes dictated by the calendar. It is necessary therefore to consider the matter of rhythm and balance in preaching.

Suppose the pastor has preached three sermons in a row emphasizing the love and acceptance of God. It may be time to inject a prophetic note, tempering the love theme with an aspect of divine judgment on the failure of the Christian community. Or suppose he or she has been preaching a series of sermons on a biblical book. It may be time for a more topical approach in which the biblical text plays its part but is not central to the degree that it was in the earlier sermons.

I have found in my own preaching that it is important to alternate between sermons that are "heavy" and sermons that are "light." If I have presented two or three sermons in a row that were very intense or that dealt with difficult or complex material, I always try to succeed them with a sermon on a gentler or more whimsical note. Following Christmas, for example, when everyone is depleted by the frantic pace of the season and I have dealt for two or three Sundays with the themes of repentance (beginning of Advent, John the Baptist) and incarnation, I may slip into a lighter mood with a sermon entitled "Pardon My Breakdown" or one called "What Do You Do for a Man Who Has Everything?"

People seem to respond to this alternation with genuine excitement, and I myself enjoy the change. For both of us, it is like an agreeable change from a routine diet, or like reading Erma Bombeck or the funny papers after a heavy front page and editorial section of the paper. Then, the next week, we are ready to return to stronger fare.

The preacher, if we reflect on it, has many emphases to make: pastoral, prophetic, ethical, biblical/theological, and evangelical, to name only a few. They are all part of the pastoral repertoire and, as such, part of the necessary accents in a year's pulpit work. We do well therefore to plan our sermon topics with an eye on all of them and not become Johnny-or-Jillian-one-notes. Even as we sit at our desks contemplating the preaching of the next six months, we should mentally commit ourselves to a suitable variety and find ourselves saying from time to time: "Uh-oh, I've got three strongly prophetic themes lined up in a row. That's pretty heavy. I'll save one of them for a later date and run in an evangelical sermon there."

TITLING SERMONS

This is perhaps as good a place as any to say a word about the titles of sermons. Some ministers, like George Buttrick, have disliked titling sermons, saying that titles tend to fall into one of two camps — either dull or cheap. John Fry, in the collection of his sermons called *Fire and Blackstone*, used primarily one-word titles: "Blindness," "Deafness," "Shame," "Soul," "Cop-Out," "Burned," "Sight," "Mercy." But well-chosen titles can serve several purposes for sermons: they help the preacher to summarize the message in his or her own mind; they stimulate the congregation's anticipation about the sermon before it is preached; and they help people to remember the sermon long after the hour of worship has passed.

Some ministers are more gifted than others in the choosing of titles. In fact, some even begin to conceive the sermon around a fascinating title that has come to mind, instead of with a text or theme to be dealt with. It is a good idea to keep a page or two in one's notebook solely for good titles one has thought of. Often they will turn into sermons over a period of months or years. Sometimes they provide a title for a sermon that evolved from another source. And even the ones that are never used help to stimulate the mind to think of other titles that are attractive and useful. The very

FUNDAMENTALS OF PREACHING

existence of a title collection in one's notebook keeps the mind at
work on the problem of finding good titles.

What makes a good title?

A good title is *interesting*. It has a certain flair, a vibrant quality,
about it. "The Doctrine of God" is a sound title, but it is not
interesting. It belongs on the spine of a heavy theological book, not
on a sermon. "The God We Would Like to Have" or "An Introduction to Thinking About God" is a much more accessible title. The
average person can become interested in it, and doesn't have the
feeling of being in for a lecture.

A good title is *reasonably brief*. It packs the central idea of the
sermon into a succinct phrase. Helen Crotwell's "Broken Community" and Clayton E. Williams's "Living Today Forever" are examples. They quickly and effectively summarize the content of the
sermons they name. As Edmund Holt Linn says, the preacher
should avoid titles like this caricature of a doctoral thesis subject:
"The Pragmatic Implications of the Recusant Political Economy as
Related to the Experience of Certain Creative Influences in Recent
Expressions of Dissociated Underprivileged Minority Social
Brotherhoods in the Middle Northeast Sector of Frazemont
County."[9]

Another mark of a good title is its *honesty*. That is, it fairly and
accurately describes the contents of the particular sermon it
represents. It is not a mere clever phrase in search of an audience.
It truly depicts the sermon to be offered by the preacher. Years ago,
when John Broadus was professor of preaching at Southern Baptist
Seminary in Louisville, he created a stir in many congregations
across the country by announcing that he would preach, in a day
of controversy over the length of women's hair, a sermon called
"Top Knot Go Down." Then Broadus would read his text, an
eschatological saying of Jesus found in Mark 13:15 and Matt. 24:17,
in which Jesus warned the disciples about the destruction of
Jerusalem, saying that in that terrible day "let him who is on the
house*top not go down* to take what is in his house." This was
thought to be very clever, but it is the kind of carnival pitch that
teaches people to be distrustful of ministers.

It is often helpful if a sermon title is *personal* in nature—if it is

178

slanted in such a way as to reveal the sermon's relevance to the hearer. This not only proves more intriguing to the congregation but keeps the preacher oriented toward the listeners while preparing and preaching the sermon. The preacher who announces the title "Salvation History" is much more likely to deliver a scholarly disquisition than the one who announces "Redemption When You Need It Most." David Ogilvy in *Confessions of an Advertising Man* tells of two friends who had a bet on whether one of them could write an ad for the *New York Times* the other would be compelled to read. The ad writer simply began his full-page ad with the name of his friend and said the ad was about him. The friend read every word! This is an important fact of communication in preaching: people are attracted by sermons that are obviously relevant to them.

Finally, a good title is *memorable*. It has a lilt or rhythm that lingers in the mind. Who could forget Fosdick's "The Importance of Doubting Our Doubts" or Ann Denham's "Care and the Uppity Woman" or Ernest Campbell's "Every Battle Isn't Armageddon"? They stick like burrs in the psyche, recalling the sermons years after they were preached. That, in the end, may be the real value of titles: they gig our minds into recollection, so that they go on working long after we hear them. The gospel in them is like reverberations from an infinitely vibrating tuning fork!

The preacher who has difficulty thinking of titles may be helped by realizing that most sermon titles fall into one of the following categories:

1. *Clever titles*. These are titles that provoke thought or offer a play on words. Examples are Garth Thompson's "The March of the Wouldn't Soldiers" and "An Aye for an Aye."

2. *Titles from books, plays, and movies*. These are especially effective during times when everyone is reading and talking about a particular book, play, or movie title. One minister preached on "Everything You Always Wanted to Know About Dying—But Were Afraid to Ask." Another took the title "The Exorcist—New Testament Version." Foy Valentine has a sermon called "You Can't Go Home Again," based on the title of Thomas Wolfe's novel. Such titles work best in highly literate communities. In those less liter-

ate, titles may be taken from television shows that most people are likely to know. One minister preached on the Cain and Abel story and called it "All in the Family."

3. *Question titles.* Unanswered questions have the virtue of making people contemplate answers before hearing the minister's sermon. Thus a title such as "Giving Thanks" can probably be made more provocative by turning it into "What Are We Thankful For?" Fosdick often used questions for titles, as in the sermons "Why Worship?" and "Are We Part of the Problem or the Answer?" Robert McCracken assembled an entire book of his sermons under the title *Questions People Ask.*

4. *Image titles.* These are titles of a pictorial nature; they give an immediate image to the mind. Sometimes the image is not so complete as to give the sermon entirely away, but is merely evocative. For example, William M. Elliott, Jr., preached a sermon on "Prayer and a Poultice," and Thomas Martin preached one called "Peanut-Butter Hands," and James W. Angell had one called "Put Your Arms Around the City." Weatherhead was fond of such concrete titles. He preached a sermon entitled "Turning the Corner" and one entitled "Key Next Door." In each of these titles, there is a specific image evoked in the mind. Many people can remember what they can *see,* and the titles help them to visualize the sermons.

5. *Good, clear titles.* This is a large category for all those titles that have nothing special about them except that they are strong and lucid—titles such as E. Stanley Jones's "Christianity and Health," Norman Vincent Peale's "The Tough-minded Optimist," Edmund Steimle's "The Peril of Ordinary Days," and Carl F. H. Henry's "The Displaced Christ and Our Disordered World." It is probably easiest for titles in this category to be leaden and dull, for they rely on no special trick to compel interest. But a title that is both apt and transparent to its message is a glory to any sermon.

6. *Personal interest titles.* These are the titles that exude a spirit of pastoral care, that seem to say to the reader or the listener, "Here is a sermon you need and will delight to hear." Fosdick and Peale are well-known masters of this kind of title. Here are some samples from Fosdick's sermons: "The Importance of the Ordinary

Man," "On Finding It Hard to Believe in God," "Making the Most of Friendship," "On Being Adequate for Life," "Handling Life's Second-Bests," "The Power of Believing You Can," and "When Life Goes All to Pieces." Titles of personal interest often begin with the words "How to . . ."—"How to Make the Most of Your Life," "How to Live Before You Die," "How to Find a Safe Place in the Storm."

THE COLLECTIVE SERMON

It is important, in planning one's pulpit work, to reflect wisely and deeply on the needs of the congregation. A good pastor will do this periodically, making lists of the kind on page 00. Then sermon emphases can be scheduled to treat these needs, both during the special days of the Christian and secular calendars and during the other Sundays of the year. No year should pass without sermons addressed to loneliness, grief, discouragement, distrust, lack of commitment, confusion, and failure.

One sure way to relate preaching to the needs and interests of the people is to secure the help of a group of parishioners in planning the sermons for a specific period of time. Browne Barr and Mary Eakin have described in a chapter of *The Ministering Congregation* how such a group in First Congregational Church of Berkeley, California, spent time together each week discussing the text for the coming Sunday and volunteering ideas and material to be used in the sermon. The minister still prepared the sermon, but the people provided much of the substance from which it was drawn.

It is also possible to use such a group without centering specifically on a text. At the first meeting of the group, the leader can suggest that the members brainstorm to determine what preaching emphases have not been heard enough in the congregation in recent months. These emphases can then become the subjects for discussion in ensuing meetings, with each becoming the focus of a sermon.

The group should be selected from a cross section of the church membership and include young and old, male and female, intellectual and non-intellectual, conservative and liberal. Members should be invited to be part of the group for a specific period of time. Six to eight weeks is an optimal time span; it is brief enough to command faithful attendance, yet long enough to provide continuity of group feelings and discussion.

The idea is to get as free and wide-ranging a discussion as possible on each issue or text considered. Members should be encouraged to introduce and talk about anything that occurs to them in the course of discussions — ideas, memories, feelings, personal anecdotes. The leader acts as a facilitator, not as an instructor. Often it is best to have an experienced group leader to perform this function, with the sessions being tape-recorded for the minister to hear. This ensures that the minister's presence is not an inhibiting factor in the group and that the discussion does not take a "religious" turn merely because the minister is there.

If the minister is present, he or she can make notes on the salient features of the discussion. If not, the minister can listen to the tape or have a secretary transcribe it for careful study. Transcription is highly desirable, for it makes the discussion more accessible for reflection than it is on tape, but it is a formidable task, as the typescript of a two-hour session often runs to fifty or sixty pages.

The day after the group meeting, while the material is fresh, the minister sits down with the list of ideas and anecdotes voiced in the discussion and begins to sort the material into usable form. The first step is a brainstorming list like the one on page 63. From there, the planning and composition of the sermon may follow by the method described on pages 65–102.

Preaching with the use of a sermon group has several distinct advantages. First, it reasserts the importance of lay involvement at all levels of ministry. Laypersons realize they have a stake in the preaching of the church as well as in the day-to-day ministry. Often they become quite excited about having contributed material for the sermon, and invariably they acquire a new understanding of how sermons come into being.

Second, it answers the problem many ministers express about not having enough material to preach about. Instead of canvassing books of sermons for usable ideas and stories, they can tap this endless resource within their own congregations.

Third, it establishes an immediate relationship between the gospel and contemporary life. There is no "relevance gap" between preaching and the human situation, because the material for sermons springs directly from people's lives. Instead of seeming remote, locked in a world of abstraction, the preacher deals with thoughts and emotions "hot from the oven of real affairs."

Fourth, it constantly revitalizes the minister's own faith. The preacher who is forever providing his or her own resources for preaching becomes spiritually empty at times and feels incapable of going on. But the chance to hear members of the group talk about their faith and interact on theological and spiritual matters dramatically renews the minister's vision, so that he or she preaches out of the overflow, not the underflow.

Fifth, the minister gets to know the group members in a way he or she probably would not if it were not for this experience, and is able to provide pastoral care to these persons at an otherwise unthinkable level. It is like having group therapy sessions in which people discuss the most important matters in their lives, and being able to follow up the stories and hints voiced in the group with genuine pastoral interest.

With regard to using in a sermon material that people have disclosed in group sessions, it is imperative that the minister make clear to the group members two caveats: (1) that they specifically identify during the sessions anything they do not wish to have repeated publicly, and (2) that the minister, being human and having more interest in some ideas than in others, will use only *some* of the ideas and anecdotes from the session, not all of them. The first warning is to prevent misunderstandings or bad feelings if the minister repeats a personal remark or story, and the second is to disarm the sensitivities of those who will listen to the sermon to see if *their* contributions have been chosen for inclusion.

While it is recommended that groups terminate after a maximum of eight or ten weeks, there is no reason not to convene other groups after the termination, so that a church might conceivably have a group meeting continuously through the year, helping the minister with the preparation of the sermon. Ministers who have tried this report two benefits from the ongoing process: the congregation is soon peppered with eager listeners who have been part of previous groups and have an unusual interest in sermons; and the people who have been part of the process before are constantly coming to the minister or present group members with ideas and material for sermons which they have discovered and would like to see incorporated into the preaching ministry of the church. In other words, there is nothing like being part of the team to build a permanent team spirit in the congregation.

REPEATING SERMONS

The preacher who plans pulpit work according to the church and secular calendars, and who supplements this with the use of sermon groups at least part of the year, should have little trouble projecting enough sermons to meet an annual quota. Even so, preachers often flag in their energies and need some workable plan for filling the quota when normal supplies do not keep up with demand. This is particularly true for ministers in churches accustomed to having Sunday evening services or midweek services in which some preaching is expected. Fosdick used to say, when he was preaching twice each Sunday, that he burned the logs in the morning and the chips at night. Some ministers might even be said to burn logs in the morning and sawdust at night!

One way to secure a little breathing space in preparation time is to repeat certain sermons that have already been preached. Most persons in the congregation are quite happy to hear certain sermons preached again. When Charles Wellborn was minister of Seventh and James Baptist Church in Waco, Texas, he had an annual "Preach It Again" month when he repreached four sermons given earlier in the year. A circular was distributed to the congregation listing all the previous sermons and asking people to indicate which ones they wished to hear again. There was always excitement about which sermons would be chosen, and large crowds attended the services when the sermons received their second preaching.

Clovis Chappell thought it a good idea to preach sermons again, especially if the minister continues to work on them to improve them. "Preaching an old sermon is bad," he said, "only if it was not worth preaching the first time."[10] Most really good preachers have shared this attitude.

Good music is not discarded once it has been sung. It is played and sung over and over, gaining new charm for its hearers each time it is repeated. Good art is not viewed once and then put in a warehouse or destroyed. It is hung where everyone can see it, to be studied again and again, and to rise in its viewers' estimation as they behold it. Admittedly, a sermon is not art in the same sense that some music and paintings are; the preacher serves an aim beyond the aesthetic commitment of the artist. Yet there is something artful about a well-made sermon. The ideas march, the phrases do their work, the illustrations release their light at proper moments, the climax is achieved and the point made with all the finesse at the command of the preacher. Why should a good sermon be abandoned once it has been preached? Who would not like to hear again Robertson or Spurgeon or Brooks preaching one of their magnificent sermons? Who would not wish to listen once more to Fosdick's great mournful voice preaching "Life Victorious Over Death," or be present to watch and hear Buttrick working his way through his Harvard sermon "Who Owns the Earth?"

The practice of repreaching sermons must not be abused, of course. But it does sometimes offer a significant breather for the minister whose mind and spirit are too exhausted to assemble a new sermon of worth. And that is a problem to which we must turn in the final chapter.

NOTES

1. Karl Barth, *The Word of God and the Word of Man*, tr. Douglas Horton (New York: Harper & Brothers, Harper Torchbooks, 1957), p. 189.

2. P. T. Forsyth, *Positive Preaching and the Modern Mind* (London: Independent Press, 1957), pp. 61–62.

3. George Sweazey, *Preaching the Good News* (Englewood Cliffs, N.J.: Prentice-Hall, 1976), p. 159.

4. James S. Stewart, *Heralds of God: A Practical Book on Preaching* (New York: Charles Scribner's Sons, 1956), p. 69.

5. Gerhard von Rad, *Biblical Interpretations in Preaching*, tr. John E. Steely (Nashville: Abingdon Press, 1977), pp. 16-18.

6. George Gibson, *Planned Preaching* (Philadelphia: Westminster Press, 1954), p. 24.

7. Albert Mollegen, *Preaching the Christian Year* (New York: Charles Scribner's Sons, 1957), p. 37.

8. Gibson, *Planned Preaching*, p. 61.

9. Edmund Holt Linn, *Preaching as Counseling: The Unique Method of Harry Emerson Fosdick* (Valley Forge, Pa.: Judson Press, 1966), p. 37.

10. Clovis Chappell, *Anointed to Preach* (Nashville: Abingdon-Cokesbury Press, 1951), p. 116.

---9---

The Person Behind
the Sermon

Preaching is an enormous responsibility. In any congregation there are dozens of people with diverse personal needs. They come in many moods, from vastly differing backgrounds, and sit there before us. Some faces are turned up in hopefulness, others in defiance. "Entertain us," say some of them. "Inform us," say others. "Feed us," say all. The preacher too is human. How can he or she meet all these requirements in a single sermon of fifteen or twenty minutes?

Even the most gifted preachers have moments when they are terrified by the task of preaching. "Why didn't I become a clerk or a truck driver?" they ask themselves. "I can never do what I ought to do as a preacher."

Fortunately the moments usually pass rather quickly. But they are frequent enough to induce a constant sense of humility in most ministers. And the older ministers become, the humbler they feel. Gone is the bumptious confidence of youth, when they knew too little to realize what limited persons they were. In its place is the sobriety of age—and, if they are lucky, a confidence of another kind, born of experience and technique, of having practiced a craft so thoughtfully for years that they can rely on what they have learned to get them through the tight places. There is no cockiness in the latter kind of confidence—only a sense of gratitude to God that it exists and suffices when the wellsprings of the spirit are not running high enough to make preaching a genuine pleasure.

There are few vocations in which the character and inner life of the persons are as important as they are in the ministry. To preach well Sunday after Sunday preachers must be in touch with the deepest resources of their beings. Their spirits must be whole and alert, sensitive to inner feelings and to the needs of others. They must be relaxed enough to draw upon all their wit and knowledge, yet excited enough to leap beyond the sum total of their powers and produce sermons that are obviously "given by God." There is no profession in which performance depends so much upon the accumulation of insight and information. Good preaching is a matter of *overflow* — of having one's mood and spirit so primed with reading and experience that they simply rise up in weekly rhythm to produce a Nilotic blessing of the environment.

"Painting," says Robert E. C. Browne, "is not merely what a painter does when he is at the canvas with a brush in his hand; the painting arises largely through what he does when he is not painting or thinking about painting."[1] If this is true of the painter, it is even more true of the preacher. The sermon is the result of so much more than the time and effort actually expended in producing it. It is the result of the preacher's entire spiritual life, the preacher's moral convictions, the preacher's personal experiences and relationships, the preacher's reading and reflection, even the preacher's health and diet.

This is why someone has spoken of "the remoter preparation" of the sermon — the part that lies, like the bulk of the iceberg, below the specific act of preparation. It is impossible to overestimate the importance of this remoter preparation. Even though it occurs unconsciously, it does much to determine the character and quality of the sermon. If ministers are hurried and thoughtless, their sermons will reflect it. If their scholarly and devotional lives are thin and impoverished, this too will show in their preaching. Shallow persons preach few deep sermons. If, on the other hand, ministers read widely, spend adequate time in prayer and reflection, and enjoy healthy relationships with their families and other persons, their sermons are bound to reveal these facts, regardless of the texts and subjects on which they preach.

It is important, then, in any consideration of preaching, to underscore the significance of the larger life of the preacher to the actual development and delivery of the sermon. In order for preaching to occur as overflow, attention must be given to the particular facets of study and experience that do most to create an overflow situation. We shall conclude our study of the craft of sermon preparation by looking at the minister's spiritual life, intellectual development, physical fitness, and interpersonal relationships.

THE MINISTER'S SPIRITUAL LIFE

"It is part of your duty," said A. J. Gossip in his Warrack Lectures, "to bring home to people that this faith of ours is not a pond round which you can stroll in half an hour, and at the end say, 'There it is, you see,' but a tremendous shoreless sea; that there are awe on awe, and mystery on mystery, and marvel upon staggering marvel heaped up in it. What does it matter about our poor little reputation if through our very stammering failure they see something of the bigness of Christ, and the amazement of God's love?"[2]

The faith *is* a "tremendous shoreless sea." There *are* "awe on awe, and mystery on mystery, and marvel upon staggering marvel heaped up in it." But it is so easy to forget! We become caught up in administrative duties, committee responsibilities, an endless round of telephone calls and letter writing, and the inevitable trivia of day-to-day existence, and before we know it these, not "marvel upon staggering marvel," lie squarely in the midst of our consciousness.

This is why it is so imperative for the minister to have a disciplined life of prayer and Bible study, of meditation and reading in the great devotional literature of the ages. Otherwise the sense of awe and mystery which first commanded his or her entrance into ministry will be forgotten in the onrush of daily affairs and the note of spiritual excitement will be hushed in both sermon and conversation.

James McCutcheon, writing his book *The Pastoral Ministry*, set a chapter on the devotional life at the very beginning. Twenty-five years in the parish ministry had convinced him, he said, of the absolute indispensability of prayer and Bible study at the center of everything the minister does. The power of a disciplined spiritual life radiates out into all the other areas of a minister's existence — counseling, preaching, parish planning, even financial administration.

Here is McCutcheon's description of his daily prayer routine:

My rule of life opens with a brief prayer of access, or invocation, and the General Confession. This is followed by twenty minutes of Bible study, ten minutes of meditating upon nonscriptural devotional literature, and twenty minutes of private prayer (during which I reflect on yesterday's failures, seek specific help for the current day's labors, pray for such civic and parish needs as lie most heavily on my heart, intercede individually for each person on my parish prayer list, and pray for each individual in my own family). I conclude by reciting the General Thanksgiving, the Apostles' Creed, and the Lord's Prayer. It has been my habit to pay close attention to the church year in the selection of readings and prayers. This imparts a refreshing variety to the exercise, as well as immersing my little part of the Kingdom work in the infinitely larger and strengthening life of the whole Christian church. Like many other past and present parish ministers, I have discovered that what happens in the first hour of my working day is alone what makes all the rest possible.[3]

Few professional persons have the minister's power to set their own working schedules. Yet most ministers make a botch of their schedules by not reserving appropriate periods of time for study and devotional practice. It is one of Parkinson's laws that the amount of time needed for any job is all the time there is, and that is precisely what ministers tend to give to the routine duties of planning, calling, counseling, and tending to the administrivia of each day. In each new parish the minister should make it immediately clear to church members that he or she sets aside certain hours of the day — preferably in the morning — for praying, reading, reflecting, and working on sermons and prayers. Our people need to know that this is important work, vital to the performance of ministry, and that it commands a vital place in our daily hours. By making this time central to our role performance, we both say something theologically about prayer and study to our people and remind ourselves of the centrality these activities should have in ministry.

Ministers who do not pray and pore over the Scriptures as a regular practice become easily discouraged by the obstacles normally encountered in ministry. Without a sense of the eternal presence, they feel depressed by minimal response to their messages, poor attendance in the services, and a general appearance of failure in their ministries. They lose the sense of miracle at the heart of New Testament faith and cease to believe any longer in the transformation of society into the kingdom of God. A pallor settles over everything they think and say and do. They begin to feel tired and listless. Instead of the sound of trumpets in their sermons, signaling hope and advancement, there is the sad, lingering note of French horns, calling retreat and death.

A minister whose spiritual life is unattended will naturally have difficulty preaching fifty or one hundred sermons a year, year in and year out for a lifetime. One sermon will sound pretty much like another, with nothing to distinguish it from the others. But the minister who reads the Bible daily and listens to the voice from its pages will never run out of fresh ideas for sermons. The minister who lives with Augustine and Bernard of Clairvaux and Thomas à Kempis and C. S. Lewis and Thomas Merton, breathing in the rarefied atmosphere of their devotional writings, will always have something valuable to say about the life of the spirit. The minister who learns to pray constantly, turning even fantasies and night dreams into material for reflection and devotion, will be like a fountain of everlasting life in the pulpit.

AN INTELLECT ON FIRE

It is often assumed by young Christians that there is a contradiction between the life of piety and the life of learning. Nothing could be farther from the truth. Many of the greatest saints of the ages have been fervent students and scholars, taking, as Bacon advised, all knowledge for their province. When R. W. Dale gave the Lyman Beecher Lectures at Yale Divinity School over a hundred years ago, he knew his words would be heard and read by many ministers formed in an anti-intellectual tradition. He cited a passage from Richard Baxter, one of the great Puritan devotionalists:

> I have looked over Hutten, Vives, Erasmus, Scaliger, Salmasius, Casaubon, and many other critical grammarians, and all Gruter's critical volumes. I have read almost all the physics and metaphysics I could hear of. I have wasted much of my time among loads of historians, chronologers, and antiquaries. I despise none of their learning; all truth is useful. Mathematics, which I have least of, I find a pretty, manlike sport. . . . I much value the method and sobriety of Aquinas, the subtlety of Scotus and Ockham, the plainness of Durandus, the solidity of Ariminensis, the profundity of Bradwardine; the excellent acuteness of many of their followers; of Aureolus, Capreolus, of Bannes, Alvarez, Zumel, &c.; of Mayro, Lychetus, Trombeta, Faber, Meurisse, Rada, &c.; of Ruiz, Pennatus, Suarez, Vasquez, &c.; of Hurtado, of Albertinus, of Lud. à Dola, and many others.[4]

It was men like Baxter, said Dale, who gave muscle and fiber to the religious life of early Protestantism. They were the ministers of a time when religious faith was most robust and when religious earnestness was most intense.

Part of the weakness of the church in our time, it is often maintained, is our lack of great scholar-preachers like Fosdick and Buttrick and Scherer, who were all preaching in New York City in the same era. Their reading was phenomenal. In every sermon they quoted historians, essayists, scientists, poets, novelists, artists, biographers, statesmen. Fosdick said in his autobiography that he began the practice early in his ministry of taking an important subject, reading everything worthwhile that had been written about it in the past fifty years, and then moving on to another subject. Buttrick, who helped to plan the monumental *Interpreter's Bible* and then edited every page of it, read at least one new book a week during the busiest years of his ministry. Scherer read constantly, keeping a hard book going in the mornings (one he had to underline and linger over) and easy ones going in the evenings. He always read his *New York Times* standing up, so he wouldn't waste time that should be devoted to his studies.

Ministers who aspire to preaching truly helpful and instructive sermons for their people cannot neglect the constant feeding of their intellects, for they can no more make bricks without straw than the ancient Israelites could. There is not as much need today for the kind of apologetics that flourished in Christian circles early in this century, whereby preachers defended the faith against a militant atheism growing out of Darwinism and the higher criticism of the Bible. But there is a need for preachers to draw on the vast resources of art and scholarship and technological understanding to assist believers in knowing how to be Christians in such a complicated time. They should not have to be Christians *over against* the kind of culture in which they live, by withdrawing from the culture and opposing its very nature. Yet, unless we provide structures of thinking for being Christian *in* the culture and converting the culture, they have no alternative. And we cannot perform this demanding task without constant reading and study, not only in the theologians of culture but in the outstanding voices of the culture itself.

When William Sloane Coffin was addressing a ministers' group in Oklahoma, several ministers confessed that they would like to be more involved in world issues such as nuclear disarmament, food for the masses, and the rights of Third World nations but simply felt inadequate because they knew so little about them. "How many of you," asked Coffin, "have read at least one book on the nuclear situation?" Only two or three hands went up in a crowd of more than a hundred ministers. "There's your answer," said Coffin. "How can you expect to know anything if you don't read?" Coffin himself reads omnivorously in the field of human rights and world management, twin themes of enormous importance in our times.

Consider some of the important areas for ministers' reading today.

1. *Human rights.* The world in general has never been more sensitive to this subject than it is today. Significant new books appear constantly on the themes of feminism, homosexuality, aging, law and justice, penology, ecology, poverty, hunger and nutrition, the distribution of energy resources, and the emergence of Third World nations. Our parishioners are interested in many of these

subjects. They need help from the pulpit to understand them in theological perspective and to know how to commit their own resources in behalf of the world beyond the parish.

2. *Scientific and technological advance.* Science doesn't change the gospel we preach, but it changes the situation in which the gospel is heard and received. Therefore ministers need to read scientific journals and books to keep abreast of the more important developments in this area. Our lives are vastly affected by new technologies. People who use computers to solve problems and to play games develop unconscious new modes of communication. A preacher who does not participate in these modes is a less effective communicator of the gospel.

3. *Medical and psychological research.* No novelist or film writer today can ignore developments in medical and psychological research and write for contemporary audiences. Neither can a preacher. As we understand more about the functioning of the human body and the human mind, we are in a better position to counsel parishioners about their personal problems and to understand how faith and physical health are related. Consider a single development in brain research: the discovery of left-brained and right-brained propensities, and the tendency of some people to be analytical while others are intuitive. This has enormous implications for typologies of human behavior and helps to explain why some people in congregations are theologically or dogmatically oriented while others are pietistically or mystically inclined.

4. *Arts, film, theater, music, and dance.* The creative arts are a vital aspect of human development in any era. We cannot hope to understand our times or our culture apart from a general knowledge of them. The arts in the twentieth century have undergone cataclysmic changes. We have witnessed cubism, expressionism, surrealism, and pop art; the theater of Beckett, Ionesco, and Arrabal; and musical performances as grandly diverse as Stravinsky's *Le Sacre du Printemps*, Bernstein's *Mass*, and Sondheim's *Sweeney Todd*. Walter Ong in *The Presence of the Word* talks about the importance of the psychological or tonal spectrum in which the eternal Word is communicated. Preachers who genuinely care about the transmission of ideas will be interested

in the way the creative spirits of our age stretch and shape the human imagination.

5. *Fiction.* Properly speaking, fiction is one of the creative arts and could have been subsumed in the previous paragraph. It is accorded a paragraph of its own for two reasons: (a) it is so completely accessible for the average minister, being available in paperback and condensations, and in every local library; and (b) it deals so obviously in wordcraft, which is part of the minister's own professional expertise. Even Jonathan Edwards, the redoubtable author of "Sinners in the Hands of an Angry God," expressed great admiration for the novels of Joseph Fielding, one of the earliest writers in the form, and said he should like to study them in order to improve his own verbal style. There is no excuse for preachers who do not steep themselves in the writings of such authors as Flannery O'Connor, Albert Camus, Kurt Vonnegut, Jr., Saul Bellow, Bernard Malamud, and James Dickey. Any minister who can read Frederick Buechner's *The Final Beast*, Margaret Craven's *I Heard the Owl Call My Name*, or Thomas Klise's *The Last Western* and not emerge a more sensitive theologian and better preacher is suffering from a premortem case of mental paralysis.

6. *Television and mass communications.* The effect of the television industry on our world and the way people feel, think, and behave today is beyond estimate. Its consequences for the gospel lie far deeper in complexity than books and seminars on the "electronic church" are able to describe. It has revolutionized communications on a global basis and changed the way people perceive their environments. McLuhan's writings are only the beginning in an attempt to understand this modern phenomenon. We shall probably not understand it by the end of the twenty-first century. But we cannot pretend interest in how people receive and process information—how they hear preaching—without attempting to learn all we can about this fascinating medium and its power in our daily lives.

7. *Travel and anthropology.* One of the big differences television has made in the world, we are told, is that ours is the first age in which people travel to foreign lands because they have already

seen them. There is truth in this. Television, along with the graphics industry, has created a global consciousness and a sense of the immediacy of even the remotest parts of the world. Still, the media are no substitute for actually visiting other lands and seeing firsthand how other peoples live. There are nuances of sight, sound, and smell that cannot be captured on film or in a travel book. A writer like Michener can describe what it is like to enter a great cathedral in Toledo, Spain; but no description can equal what a traveler feels upon walking into cool, dark recesses of that vaulted building and smelling the incense rising like holy perfume among the El Grecos and the elaborate carvings of the ancient reredos. The minister who preaches in today's world ought to be both traveler and reader, a citizen of the world in the fullest sense. Dale sensed this a century ago and tried to convert the imaginations of his audience at Yale:

> There are some preachers whose sermons — whatever they are preaching about — remind one of the conversation of people that have never been outside the village or the county in which they were born; people who would settle the affairs of a great nation in the interests of their own particular parish, and with no other knowledge than that which they have acquired in discussing and managing their own parochial business.[5]

We should know the world as thoroughly as we can, through actual visits and through reading. We should study the literatures, cultures, and religions of people in other nations. One of the saddest omissions in many seminary curricula today is of the study of world religions. Our people could learn so much about discipline from the Muslims, so much about prayer and meditation from the Zen Buddhists, so much about awe and mystery from adherents of certain African religions. There is an unforgivable combination of fear and pride in our Christian insularism.

8. *Sociology and ethics.* With the advent of urban culture, mass communications, convenient travel, and technicized industry, human life has undergone dramatic changes. Churches occupy a lower place in society than they once did. Values and standards of

behavior have shifted. We live in a new age of sexual permissive-ness. Pornography, crime, and drug abuse are widespread. New techniques in the medical field suggest the possibility of alterations in life patterns through a variety of interventions such as genetic control, brain implants, and life termination. Hosts of questions about society and the individual remain unresolved. Many of these have direct ethical and moral implications. Clergypersons are expected to give guidance to their congregations. Only by wide reading and constant reflection can they hope to provide respon-sible direction as people face the difficult decisions of coming decades.

9. *Biblical and theological studies.* Far too many parish preach-ers leave the weightier treatises on biblical and theological subjects to scholars in seminaries and universities, when they should be wrestling with the meaning of these treatises themselves. A semi-nary education is not meant to complete our education for minis-try, but to *initiate* it. Biblical languages are not intended as stumbling blocks along the route to a theological degree, but as tools for the rest of our lives. A parish minister who does not keep up with advances in biblical and theological work during the whole of his or her lifetime is as shameless as a medical doctor who does not return to medical school for frequent refresher seminars in the latest medical discoveries and techniques. We cannot do our work well without being biblical theologians. And we cannot be biblical theologians without constantly studying and reflecting on the best scholarship in the field.

The beauty of reading is that it is a chance to spend hours and days in the company of authors we choose. They have distilled onto the pages of their books the essence of their thinking and feeling and have shaped it as pleasantly as they can. They have garnered facts, ideas, and images that would require years for us to assemble on our own. In a single day we can reflect on archaeological find-ings with Loren Eiseley, survey all the scholarship on the Gospel of John with Raymond Brown, visit a monastery with Henri Nouwen, and behold the majesty of a sunset in the Greek isles with Lawrence Durrell. Books are the magic carpet of the mind: in the

197

twinkling of an eye they whisk us away to the most marvelous thoughts and experiences, then deposit us again right where we were sitting, ready to turn to the next task of the day.

THE MINISTER'S HEALTH
AND RECREATION

People commonly joke that ministers have little to do, working only one day in seven. In fact, there are few jobs so demanding as the ministry. The duties of the calling are so comprehensive, and the hours so variable, that the average clergyperson probably has less time for self-interest and self-repair each week than almost anyone in the congregation. There are always things to be done— visits to the hospital and to shut-ins, calls on prospective members, committee meetings, planning sessions with the staff, funerals, weddings, counseling sessions, the preparation of liturgies, prayers, and sermons — not to mention keeping abreast of scholarship, reading for self-improvement, and taking time to pray and meditate. Many ministers have found in recent stress and tension clinics that they work under almost constant anxiety lest they fail to do their jobs well.

The subject of the minister's health may seem very remotely related to the quality of preaching, but the two are actually intimately associated. Modern communication studies have shown that far more is transmitted in any speech than the overt content of the message. In addition to that, there is a covert content, a hidden message that is often unconscious even to the speaker. If the speaker is tired or bored with the audience, this is often conveyed in small, nearly unnoticeable signals. If the speaker feels smug or superior to the audience, this too is conveyed. The nuances of feeling and meaning are there, and sometimes they add up to far more than the speaker is deliberately saying.

The gospel we preach is about redemption and wholeness. The word *salus*, from which we get "salvation," means *health*. Suppose we are preaching about wholeness and reconciliation but actually conveying a message about fragmentedness and despondency. The words may sound right, but there is something about the tune, about the look in our eyes, about the tension lines in our faces, that counters what we are saying. At best, people get a double message.

It is very important, therefore, for the preacher to be as healthy and joyous as possible. Anything less impedes his or her message about the life-giving community of God. We are working at our preaching, for this reason, even when we are taking care of ourselves.

Individuals vary, of course, and what is healthful for one may be anathema to the system of another. One will work productively in the morning, when the air is fresh, and another will work well at night, when the chores of the day are done. One will work best under pressure, when deadlines come regularly as the pages of the calendar. Another will abhor deadlines and so accomplish everything well in advance of them. But, for what they are worth, here are some suggestions for staying reasonably healthy and vigorous in the pursuit of one's ministry.

1. *Establish a suitable rhythm between work and relaxation.* Learn to work at your hardest jobs in a concentrated fashion for as long as you can profitably endure that way, then ease into less difficult work or into rest and idleness. When you have recuperated from the exertion, you can return to the concentration. Since preparing the sermon is for most ministers the most arduous or taxing work they do, it is a good idea to give your most productive time of the day to this, then switch to less demanding tasks or to some form of relaxation. By far the majority of great preachers have spent their mornings at books and sermons, then given their afternoons to visits, meetings, and other parish duties. Returning to their offices from an afternoon at the hospital or conducting a funeral, they have often felt like working again at some writing task, such as preparing pastoral prayers or litanies.

2. *Get a proper amount of physical exercise.* Ministers who do not know how to control their schedules are prone to neglect their bodies. The host of things to be done soon usurps their time for walking, running, swimming, playing tennis, or engaging in some other sport. Before they know it they are overweight or out of con-

dition, and exercise has become painful and unpleasant. Remember how constantly Paul used athletic images to speak about the Christian faith. It is an active, dynamic faith. It is not fully represented by bookish, nonathletic servants. A body kept in proper tone and condition means a mind that functions clearly and efficiently. I have often found, when a sermon was going sluggishly, that a swim or a few sets of tennis helped it to come around amazingly.

3. *Maintain a suitable diet.* "You are what you eat," says a popular slogan. Ministers are no freer to flout the laws of nutrition than anyone else. Unfortunately we probably face a larger number of club luncheons, tea parties, church dinners, and offers of occasional refreshment than most people and must learn to be both diplomatic and sensible about calories. If the body is the temple of the Holy Spirit, it should not be stuffed with junk foods and unnecessary desserts. An athlete eats to serve performance; so should a minister. But, as the performances are not the same, neither are the diets. Heavy meals and snacks call the blood into the stomach when it should be in the brain, thinking about sermons and ministry.

4. *Get a reasonable amount of sleep.* Our bodies need rest in order to do their repair work. So do our psyches. Anyone who denies this need will pay a toll in terms of sluggishness, anxiety, and irritability. A head that should be clear for thinking will be cloudy with tiredness. Some people manage on very little sleep, it is true. Thomas Edison took catnaps every four hours and worked around the clock. But most of us are constituted to need seven or eight hours of sleep a night and will not function well if we do not get it. Many persons are helped to sleep well by having a quiet time before going to bed and turning off the lights—some pray and meditate, some sit before a fire and daydream, some chat with their wives or husbands, some read a book. Watching a tense movie on television or listening to the latest news reports of atrocities and conflicts is not recommended as a prelude to peaceful slumber.

5. *Take frequent vacations.* If nightly sleep helps to repair the body and the mind for day-to-day activities, vacations help to

repair them over the long haul. Most ministers do not take vacations in the way other people do, who are able to forget the office or the household while they lie on the sand at St. Petersburg or trudge through castles on the Rhine. Their minds are often busy planning ahead to the next season's sermons or budget campaign. Frank Bauman, minister of the Foundry United Methodist Church in Washington, D.C., outlines his entire year's sermons during his two-month summer vacation. For this reason, churches need to be generous in the amount of vacation time they give their preaching ministers. Even so, the change of pace experienced in a vacation is important to the minister's well-being. For some ministers, several brief vacations are preferred to a single longer one. A week's trip to the mountains in the spring, to the shore in the summer, and to the foliage in the autumn can be cumulatively more restorative than three weeks spent at either place in one visit.

6. *Learn to play every day.* Playing is what we do naturally, without strain or tension. It is being ourselves, drifting with our emotions, enjoying the moment. People at play drop their masks, stop worrying about performance ratings, and become who they really are. Grown-ups often forget how to play. They have been schooled to react to life according to certain codes. They are so busy earning a living and trying to meet the requirements of their jobs that they lose the spirit of playfulness. Many learn to relax only when they are drinking or watching a ball game. It is important for the minister to discover the secrets of true relaxation in everyday living. Prayer and meditation is a good place to begin. The soul that is happy in God is relaxed in daily affairs. Being open and natural before God enables us to live openly and naturally before others. We stop trying to fulfill mere role expectations in ministry and find motivation for genuine ministry to others. Then we can sing and laugh and play as we go through the day — or openly weep and lament, if we feel those emotions. In short, we stay in touch with ourselves at the deepest level and are able to live simply and fully through the activities and encounters of our lives. When we go home at night, we can be fully present to our families and not preoccupied with coping situations. We can swing immediately into a ball game or an afternoon in the country,

because we do not need thirty-six hours of debriefing and deprogramming in order to enjoy the experience. It is no special honor to be known as a minister who is always earnest and on call; people who really understand about life will think you a fool or a bore — or both. And as for the relationship of playing to the sermon — creating the sermon is a playful act. That is, the mind "plays" with various ideas and ways of putting those ideas together. If it is unable to play, the sermon will be tedious indeed. And the connection is this: the minister who is a regular player, who lives naturally every day, will invariably prepare and deliver better sermons than the minister who is uptight and cannot play. What is more, the playful minister will live longer and enjoy ministry more.

Henry Ward Beecher summed it up well, though his failure to include women must be forgiven as an accident of his times:

> Men are said to have genius. What is genius but a condition of fiber, and a condition of health in fiber? It is nothing in the world but automatic thinking. And what is automatic thinking? It is thought that *thinks itself*, instead of being run up or worried up to think. Whoever thinks without thinking is in fact a genius. In music, it is said that it "makes itself." In arithmetic or mechanics, the demonstration "comes" to you. You do not think it out, except automatically. Real thinking ought to be automatic action, and almost unconscious. Under such circumstances, your intuitions and your sudden automatic thinking, nine times out of ten, will be true; and when you send slow-footed Logic afterward to measure the footsteps and the way over which your thoughts have traveled, Logic will come back and report, "Well, I did not believe it, but he was right, after all." So, then, for sharpness and accuracy and complexity of thinking, in which much of your life ought to lie, you require the best conditions of health in the system by which you think.[6]

THE MINISTER'S PERSONAL RELATIONSHIPS

Finally we come to the matter of the minister's family and personal relationships. There are few resources, outside the Bible and prayer, as important to preaching as this one. The preacher who had not learned to depend upon it has lived in unnecessary poverty of the spirit. Many of the remarks that follow will assume the married status of the clergy, but even clergypersons who are unmarried may read them in terms of their relationships to parents, siblings, and a network of friends. Persons of extreme aloofness and aloneness like Søren Kierkegaard may occasionally be of great usefulness to the church with their wit and insight. But, by and large, the church needs pastors and preachers who exist in a nexus of healthy interchange with other persons, for these provide the real models of community that enable us to move always in the direction of the community of God.

There is nothing like a close observation of family life to teach us the various truths of human nature. D. T. Niles of Sri Lanka was preaching once about jealousy and competitiveness. His text had been the Cain and Abel story from Genesis. "We have bananas growing in our backyard," he said, "free for the picking. Every morning my wife lays a banana by each plate at the breakfast table. Every morning it is the same: the children *measure* their bananas to see who got the longest and who the shortest." The congregation laughed—and understood. An illustration from Niles's own table had made the Cain and Abel narrative more real, more contemporary with their own lives.

It would surely be impossible to know the many meanings of love and suffering contained in the gospel if we didn't experience them ourselves in the context of the family and personal relationships. Shortly after my first son was born, I dedicated a book to him. I remember the form of dedication I wanted to use, but didn't because it seemed too presumptuous. It said, "I understand God better now that we are both fathers." It was true. I did understand better. I knew what it meant for God to be called Abba—Daddy—an Aramaic form of familiar address, and for God to desire good things for God's children, and for God to give rules to live by, and for God to grieve when the children did not respond in joy and goodwill.

Many people think the finest sermon the great A. J. Gossip ever preached was one he gave after his wife died. It was called "When Life Tumbles In—What Then?" The sorrowing preacher defined the magnitude of his loss in terms of the love he had felt for his wife and what she had meant to him throughout their life together. Then he turned to a fresh consideration of what it meant for God to give an only begotten son to die on the cross, and set his own loss in the context of that one. There was not a dry cheek in the church, or an unrepentant heart.

But it is not only added understanding from family life that enriches our preaching, it is the whole dimension of growth and support that enriches it. It is the sense of being an integral part of a larger entity and receiving gifts of love and regard from that entity. It is a matter of having one's very personhood enlarged by associations within the family and circle of friends, so that the preacher behind the sermon is wiser, stronger, and more compassionate than before.

Sometimes it is said that ministers should not develop close personal friendships among the members of their own congregations — that this transgresses the sense of impartiality people think the minister should display toward everyone. Fortunately this attitude seems to be disappearing. The minister's humanness is important, and congregations are learning to value it. We all need intimate friends — persons with whom to share our hopes and aspirations, our disappointments and frustrations, our little joys and triumphs. These friends strengthen and enrich us in countless ways. They make our preaching more vital and resonant. They help us to understand the gospel.

Ministers are regrettably prone, because of their multiple involvements with the congregation, to neglect their relationships with both family and friends. Dickens's Mrs. Jellyby, whose own children went about in tatters and dirt while she campaigned for the children of savages in Africa, is hardly unique in her failure to remember the old adage, "Charity begins at home." Ministers' children are often lonely and resentful of the time their parents spend caring for other persons. Ministers' husbands and wives are frequently depressed and bewildered by the feeling that they have been all but deserted by their spouses.

Wise ministers invest much of themselves in the lives of family and friends, realizing that two-way relationships have great sustaining power not only for their lives as individuals but for their psyches as preachers. They know they must be "givers" as well as

THE PERSON BEHIND THE SERMON

"takers" in the relationships—that the giving enables them to grow and, by some mysterious law of multiplication, to have more to give to members of the congregation. Perceptive clergymen take time to court their wives, take them out for candlelight dinners alone, go on frequent little trips with them; smart clergywomen remember to stroke their husbands' egos, give birthday parties for them, and prepare special meals for them. Both sexes of clergy, if they are thoughtful, spend evenings with their children, plan fun events around them on days out of school, play ball with them, and make a point of being available to talk about the things that matter to growing youngsters.

It all has to do with what psychologists call Gestalt—the total pattern of things. Or with what Jesus said about a bad tree's not being able to produce good fruit. The preacher who tries to talk about the gospel of love and redemption while his or her own personal relationships are in shambles is bound to sound a little phony. Maybe the phoniness won't come through in the words themselves, but it will come through in dozens of other ways. It can't be completely hidden. People aren't that easily fooled. Sometimes their minds are fooled. But their instincts aren't. Intuitively—below the line of consciousness—they know there is something wrong with the minister's sermon, that it doesn't quite ring true.

THE SUM OF IT ALL

What it all comes down to, in the end, is the total relationship of everything the minister *is* and *does* to what is said in the sermon. Bishop Quayle is right: in the final analysis, the art of preaching is to make a preacher and deliver that. Nothing else will suffice. All great preachers have understood this. What the old hymn says about love is also true of preaching: "Love so amazing, so divine, demands my soul, my life, my all." Fosdick spoke of preaching as drenching the congregation in one's life's blood. He knew. He oriented everything in his life—his creative energies, his family and personal relationships, his scholarly work, his counseling activities, everything—toward that one great act on Sunday morning, of preaching the gospel in a way to give hope and life to all those sitting under the sound of his voice. He didn't *merely* preach. He had an extraordinarily full life, as anyone can see by reading his autobiography, *The Living of These Days*. But everything in his life—his own devotional spirit, his great intellectual vigor, his robust physical presence, his rich personal relationships—contributed to the preparation and delivery of his sermons.

Those of us who wish to preach and preach well must order our lives so that the same is true for us. There is not one rule for some and another rule for others. We are all under the same ordination and stand under the same tradition. We all worship the same God and receive the same Spirit. And, when we get to the bottom line, there is only one way to preach—with everything we have and are.

NOTES

1. Robert E. C. Browne, *The Ministry of the Word* (Philadelphia: Fortress Press, 1976), p. 18.
2. A. J. Gossip, *In Christ's Stead* (London: Hodder & Stoughton, 1925), pp. 167–68.
3. James McCutcheon, *The Pastoral Ministry* (Nashville: Abingdon Press, 1978), p. 17.
4. In R. W. Dale, *Nine Lectures on Preaching* (New York: Barnes, 1878), pp. 109–110.
5. Ibid., p. 69.
6. Henry Ward Beecher, *Yale Lectures on Preaching*, p. 186.

An Annotated
Bibliography

Brooks, Phillips. *Eight Lectures on Preaching.* London: SPCK, 1959. The great New England preacher's Lyman Beecher Lectures of 1877 remain one of the most readable and inspiring volumes on preaching ever penned. They deal with elements both practical and personal, and propound Brooks's famous dictum that preaching is "truth through personality." Especially strong on relationship of pastoral ministry to preaching.

Browne, Robert E. C. *The Ministry of the Word.* Philadelphia: Fortress Press, 1976. Deeply theological ponderings on the calling of the preacher. Especially recommended for brighter students and those who have served in the ministry a few years. Sees the relationship between preaching and poetry, and the importance of finding one's own style and message.

Buechner, Frederick. *Telling the Truth: The Gospel as Tragedy, Comedy and Fairy Tale.* San Francisco: Harper & Row, 1977. The novelist-preacher's Lyman Beecher Lectures plead for the "enfleshing" of the gospel in words and attitudes that are real and meaningful. He contends that the preacher's task is "to create images of life through which we can somehow see into the wordless truth of our lives." Without calling attention to them, gives excellent examples of how to make the gospel story come alive.

Claypool, John R. *The Preaching Event.* Waco, Tex.: Word Books, 1980. Lyman Beecher Lectures with accent on "confessional" preaching. Extremely helpful analysis of the personal dimension of preaching, with an account of how the author first discovered the power of preaching that reveals the preacher's own struggles.

Cox, James W. *A Guide to Biblical Preaching.* Nashville: Abingdon Press, 1976. Fine handbook on an important subject. Advises: "Get as much of the form of the sermon as you can from the form of the text." Especially helpful and clear for beginning preachers.

Craddock, Fred B. *As One Without Authority: Essays on Inductive Preaching.* Enid, Okla.: Phillips University Press, 1971; reissued, Nashville: Abingdon Press, 1978. Excellent treatment of the importance of the inductive method in preaching, by which the preacher invokes the cooperation of the congregation as he or she wrestles with an idea or theme in the sermon.

Farmer, Herbert H. *The Servant of the Word.* Philadelphia: Fortress Press, 1964. Inspirational discussions of the personal dimensions of the preacher's calling, by an eminent British theologian and preacher. Also an interesting chapter on "The Need for Concreteness" in preaching. Originally given as the Warrack Lectures on preaching.

Forsyth, P. T. *Positive Preaching and the Modern Mind.* London: Independent Press, 1957. Lyman Beecher Lectures with strong emphasis on theology of preaching and preaching of theology. Although originally published in 1907, the book bristles with insights and memorable statements, and deserves rereading by every minister today.

Howe, Reuel L. *Partners in Preaching: Clergy and Laity in Dialogue.* New York: Seabury Press, 1967. Small book dealing with the crisis in preaching today. Summarizes research among laity revealing their suggestions for stronger preaching. Good emphasis on learning to preach out of one's weaknesses and doubts as well as one's strengths.

Jensen, Richard A. *Telling the Story: Variety and Imagination in Preaching.* Minneapolis: Augsburg Publishing House, 1980. Possibly the best book on preaching as storytelling. Deals with three types of preaching: *didactic* preaching, *proclamatory* preaching, and *story* preaching. Concludes that story preaching elicits more inner response from congregations than other kinds. Includes examples of author's own sermons under each category.

Keck, Leander E. *The Bible in the Pulpit: The Renewal of Biblical Preaching.* Nashville: Abingdon Press, 1978. Extremely clear and helpful examination of the problem of doing biblical preaching in a day of biblical criticism. Includes three of the author's sermons as examples of letting the text speak with its own peculiar authority.

Malcomson, William L. *The Preaching Event.* Philadelphia: Westminster Press, 1968. Casually written, absorbing study of preaching as an "event" or nexus of factors, each of which must receive consideration for successful communication. Filled with good insights.

Nichols, J. Randall. *Building the Word: The Dynamics of Communication and Preaching.* San Francisco: Harper & Row, 1980. Brilliantly written exposition of the preacher's craft from a communications viewpoint. Especially helpful for preachers with a few years' experience in the pulpit — a good "renewal" book. Insightful and practical.

Ong, Walter J. *The Presence of the Word: Some Prolegomena for Cultural and Religious History.* New Haven: Yale University Press, 1967; reissued, New York: Simon & Schuster, Clarion Books, 1970. Brilliant meditations or essays on the nature of human speech and its relationship to preaching. Combines psychology, philosophy, communications insights for profound observations on the speech-hearing continuum.

Scherer, Paul. *The Word God Sent.* New York: Harper & Row, 1965. Lectures and sermons by one of America's greatest preachers. Challenges readers to stronger theological content in sermons and to preaching the gospel with both credibility and relevance. Written in the magnificent prose and cadences with which Scherer characteristically spoke.

Steimle, Edmund A.; Niedenthal, Morris J.; and Rice, Charles L. *Preaching the Story.* Philadelphia: Fortress Press, 1980. Helpful reflections on the story quality of preaching by three outstanding preacher-homileticians. Each section of the book features a sermon for illustration and diagnosis. Particularly good for seasoned preachers who wish to rethink their approach to preaching.

Stewart, James S. *Heralds of God: A Practical Book on Preaching.* New York: Charles Scribner's Sons, 1956. Eloquent, inspiring book by one of the great preachers of our time. Five chapters — on "The Preacher's World," "The Preacher's Theme," "The Preacher's Study," "The Preacher's Technique," and "The Preacher's Inner Life"— teem with memorable statements and helpful advice.

Young, Robert D. *Be Brief About It: Clues to Effective Preaching.* Philadelphia: Westminster Press, 1980. Deftly written book about the importance of brevity in sermons today. Applies the law of physics, "To compress is to heat," to the art of preaching. Gives ten guidelines for briefer preaching, including thinking small, adopting a poetry model, selecting a simple unity, and staying close to the original inspiration for the sermon. Appends four of the author's own sermons as models of compression.

Index